CAMBRIDGE LIBRARY COLLECTION

Books of enduring scholarly value

Naval and Military History

This series includes accounts of sea and land campaigns by eye-witnesses and contemporaries, as well as landmark studies of their social, political and economic impacts. The series focuses mainly on the period from the Renaissance to the end of the Victorian era. It includes major concentrations of material on the American and French revolutions, the British campaigns in South Asia, and nineteenth-century conflicts in Europe, such as the Peninsular and Crimean Wars. Although many of the accounts are semi-official narratives by senior officers and their relatives, the series also includes alternative viewpoints from dissenting leaders, servicemen in the lower ranks, and military wives and civilians caught up in the theatre of war.

Naval Warfare with Steam

Sir Howard Douglas (1776–1861) fought in the Napoleonic wars in Spain, taught at the Royal Military College, served as lieutenant-governor of New Brunswick, lord high commissioner of the Ionian Islands, and as a Conservative M.P. for Liverpool. A military scholar, fellow of the Royal Geographical Society and Royal Society and associate of the Institution of Naval Architects, he wrote widely on bridges, systems of defence and attack, and on Britain's North American provinces. Written in retirement, when Douglas became an unofficial advisor to a succession of prime ministers, this work addresses the use of steam to propel ships, with detailed analysis of design, steering, propeller and paddle engineering and considerations of speed and manoeuvrability. The book goes on to examine tactics, including breaking the line, fuel economy and fleet arrangement. Built upon by others, this important work, first published in 1858, remains of interest to military historians.

Cambridge University Press has long been a pioneer in the reissuing of out-of-print titles from its own backlist, producing digital reprints of books that are still sought after by scholars and students but could not be reprinted economically using traditional technology. The Cambridge Library Collection extends this activity to a wider range of books which are still of importance to researchers and professionals, either for the source material they contain, or as landmarks in the history of their academic discipline.

Drawing from the world-renowned collections in the Cambridge University Library and other partner libraries, and guided by the advice of experts in each subject area, Cambridge University Press is using state-of-the-art scanning machines in its own Printing House to capture the content of each book selected for inclusion. The files are processed to give a consistently clear, crisp image, and the books finished to the high quality standard for which the Press is recognised around the world. The latest print-on-demand technology ensures that the books will remain available indefinitely, and that orders for single or multiple copies can quickly be supplied.

The Cambridge Library Collection brings back to life books of enduring scholarly value (including out-of-copyright works originally issued by other publishers) across a wide range of disciplines in the humanities and social sciences and in science and technology.

Naval Warfare
with Steam

HOWARD DOUGLAS

CAMBRIDGE UNIVERSITY PRESS

Cambridge, New York, Melbourne, Madrid, Cape Town,
Singapore, São Paolo, Delhi, Mexico City

Published in the United States of America by Cambridge University Press, New York

www.cambridge.org
Information on this title: www.cambridge.org/9781108053990

© in this compilation Cambridge University Press 2013

This edition first published 1858
This digitally printed version 2013

ISBN 978-1-108-05399-0 Paperback

ON

NAVAL WARFARE

WITH

STEAM.

NAVAL WARFARE

WITH

STEAM.

Dedicated, by Special Permission, to

FIELD-MARSHAL HIS ROYAL HIGHNESS THE PRINCE CONSORT, K.G.,

&c., &c., &c.

BY

GENERAL SIR HOWARD DOUGLAS, Bart.,

G.C.B., G.C.M.G., D.C.L., F.R.S.,

AUTHOR OF A 'TREATISE ON NAVAL GUNNERY,' ETC.

LONDON:
JOHN MURRAY, ALBEMARLE STREET.
1858.

LONDON : PRINTED BY W. CLOWES AND SONS, STAMFORD STREET,
AND CHARING CROSS.

TO FIELD-MARSHAL

HIS ROYAL HIGHNESS THE PRINCE CONSORT, K.G.,

&c.,   &c.,   &c.

SIR,

Authorized and honoured by your Royal Highness's gracious permission to dedicate to your Royal Highness this attempt to treat of a subject of vital importance to the country with which your Royal Highness is happily associated and identified, I have only to hope that my endeavour to give unity of system to the tactics of war by land and sea, as well as military strength to the formations of fleets, by applying the principles which regulate the dispositions and movements of armies to the new system of warfare on the ocean, for which this country ought to be fully prepared, may not be considered unworthy of the illustrious name by which my humble efforts are patronized, and not altogether useless to that great branch of Her Majesty's Service, on the efficiency and the supremacy of which the security of the Insular and Colonial Empire of Great Britain, must ever depend.

I have the honour to be,

SIR,

With sentiments of the most profound respect,

Your Royal Highness's devoted and

Most obedient humble servant,

THE AUTHOR.

INTRODUCTION.

We are now at the commencement of a new era in naval warfare, in consequence of the introduction of steam as a propelling power for ships, and its application, by all the maritime powers of Europe, to vessels of war, from those of the lowest class to line-of-battle ships of the greatest magnitude. This new power will necessarily modify, and, to a great extent, overturn, the present tactics of war on the ocean.

Hitherto the execution of naval evolutions has depended on atmospherical conditions, and often the best concerted plans for attack or defence at sea have been frustrated, when at the point of being successfully carried out, by sudden calms, or by unforeseen changes in the direction of the wind; while now, an elaborate system of appropriate machinery, put in motion by the expansive force of steam, by enabling a vessel to be moved at pleasure, with more or less rapidity, or to be brought to a state of rest, or again, to have the direction of its motion changed through the guiding power of the helm, will enable the commander of a ship or fleet to put in practice, without risk of failure, whatever manœuvre he may have determined on, whether for coming to action, or for counteracting the measures taken by his opponent, previously to, or during, all the battle movements of the fleet.

It is generally supposed that the present naval supremacy of Great Britain is mainly due to circumstances arising out of the particular nature of the moving power by which the evolutions of vessels, singly or in fleets, have been performed. That moving power is the wind acting on the sails of the ships—a power in its nature very variable ; and it is evident that the introduction of steam, as a propelling power, whose action is entirely under the control of the engineer, will bring about great changes in the relative conditions of British and foreign navies, affecting, in consequence, the maritime importance of the several European nations.

This subject has already attracted the notice of scientific men in foreign countries ; and an opinion prevails abroad, that the employment of steam as a moving power for ships of war will be attended with results beneficial to the nations of the Continent, while it will operate to the disadvantage of Great Britain.[a]

It is supposed that to superior tactical skill in our commanders, in anticipating the effects likely to arise from variations in the force and direction of the wind, and to the superior practical experience and expertness of our operative seamen in executing the orders of the officers, with respect to the manipulation of the rigging and sails, the British navy is in a great measure indebted for the success which has hitherto attended it in the hostile collisions of its ships with those of other nations ;

---

[a] " Des machines puissantes du genre d'un moteur obéissant rendra inutiles et la marine et les marins à voile dont la Grande Bretagne est un ruche si féconde."—*Des Propulsions Sous-Marins*, par M. Labrouse, 1843.

" Ce changement rendra l'expérience et les habitudes navales moins utiles, et tournera à l'avantage de la France bien plus que de l'Angleterre."—Paixhans, *Sur une Arme Nouvelle Maritime*, p. 28.

" La vapeur menaçait l'Angleterre de mettre la marine à la portée de tout grand peuple qui aurait des soldats aguerris et des finances prospérés. . . . . La vapeur, pénétrons-nous bien de cette vérité, place la question de suprématie maritime sur un terrain plus abordable pour nous."—De la Gravière, *Guerres Maritimes*, vol. ii. pp. 256, 264.

and it is observed that when the complicated manœuvres required to govern the motion of a ship under sail shall be superseded by the more simple management of steam machinery, naval warfare under steam will be in a great measure independent of nautical skill and good practical seamanship, and that the evolutions of a fleet will be reduced almost to the precision of military movements in the field.   It is hence argued that on the employment of steam-propulsion for ships of war becoming general in Europe, that supremacy which our warlike navy has so long and so happily for us maintained, will cease to exist, and that other nations, less rich in nautical resources, but more abundant in those, both personal and material, which are required for military service on land, will become relatively more powerful than they were under the former conditions.

But does it necessarily follow that Great Britain will no longer maintain her present superiority in naval warfare? or, if so, will her decline be wholly due to the employment of steam-propulsion in ships of war? The author ventures to think that such an opinion is unfounded, and that it can have been formed only on the presumption that our nautical science and mechanical skill are to remain stationary, while those of other nations go on improving.   In this case there would, indeed, come a time when the superiority would be on the Continental side, but nothing appears, at present, to justify such a presumption.   Our seamen of all ranks, are admitted to have, at this time, greater skill than those of other nations, not only in naval evolutions under sail, but also in the management of steam-machinery ; and they continue to be diligently trained in all that relates to naval tactics with wind or steam : thus they are prepared to avail themselves of every improvement that science and practice can suggest for the augmentation of their professional attainments.

This circumstance alone, *cæteris paribus*, should enable British commanders to preserve their present superiority over those of the Continent; but how much greater are the advantages of our country, in respect of its seamen, over every other nation! Foreign seamen being taken, chiefly by conscription, from towns or fields, have seldom more than that training which can be given them in ships of war, on board of which they serve almost wholly within the limits of the European waters; whereas our sailors, exerting the energies of a people long habituated to maritime pursuits, are trained in our vast mercantile marine to the performance of their duties in every region of the earth, while employed in transporting merchandise between the mother country and its widely extended colonial dominions.

Our superiority holds good also with respect to their training in the employment of steam. The machinery for the propulsion of a British steamer is the best that can be executed, and the engineers who attend it are well known to have greater skill and more experience than men of the like class in other nations; Englishmen are, in fact, generally employed to work the engines on board of the mercantile steamers of foreign countries; and no reason can be given why their skill and their energies should be stationary, or not keep pace with their increasing opportunities for improvement.

It may, therefore, be safely affirmed that the advantages which Great Britain has so long enjoyed in her maritime superiority, will rather be increased than lessened under the new and as yet untried power of motion; and it may be reasonably supposed that other nations will continue to follow rather than lead us in the career of nautical warfare. The subject is, however, one of momentous importance to us, and it should engage us to bring every possible consideration to bear on the means by which Great Britain may, even at the outset, be enabled to maintain that superiority in steam-warfare, which has already been obtained for her by the skill and intrepidity of the officers and seamen of her glorious sailing navy.

New discoveries in the means and implements of war have at all times been necessarily attended, both in fleets and armies, by new formations in the array of battle, and by modifications, or entire changes, in their tactical evolutions. The greatest change in these respects took place at the epoch of the first employment of gunpowder in warfare; but every improvement in arms has, since that time, constantly led to counteracting measures being taken in organization and movements both naval and military, of which the history of military science affords abundant examples. It must be observed, however, that alterations in tactics have always been made by slow degrees, and have generally followed at long intervals the improvements which rendered them necessary. At the present time it may be said that no efficient change has yet been made in military tactics to meet the introduction of the improved rifle as a general arm for the infantry of the line.

The employment of steam as a motive power in the warlike navies of all maritime nations, is a vast and sudden change in the means of engaging in action on the seas, which must produce an entire revolution in naval warfare, and must render necessary the immediate adoption of new measures in tactics, and new material resources; these should be forthwith studied, and provided, with all the mental and physical energies which the talent and wealth of this country can exert; in particular, no money should be spared, considering the magnitude of the object at stake,—no less than the preservation of our naval supremacy,—in procuring all that is necessary to meet the requirements of the service at this momentous epoch.

The changes which political events have produced in the maritime affairs of all the nations of Europe, and the great improvements which have been made in naval constructions and armaments, and particularly the introduction of steam as a motive power since the termination of the wars arising from the great French Revolution, are matters with which it behoves the statesmen of this country to be thoroughly acquainted. One great naval power in Europe has disappeared as such, and another has sprung up in the New World. The steam fleet of France is in a state of progressive augmentation; the government of that country having acted upon the decision of its " *Commission d'Enquête*," of 1849,[a] and has now attained a very formidable degree of strength. The division of the Russian fleet now in the Baltic, amounting to about 40 sail of the line, will speedily become a steam fleet; and the navies of the minor powers, Denmark, Sweden, and Holland, under the able administrations of those countries, are in a very efficient state. In short, the navies of Europe and of America have so increased in the number and strength of the ships, and their *personnel*, in all that relates to the science and practice of war, that, in a future contest, the sea will become the theatre of events, more important and decisive than have ever yet been witnessed.

---

[a] See the Enquête Parlementaire, sur la Situation et l'Organization des Services de la Marine Militaire, ordonnée par la Loi du 31 Octobre, 1849.' Paris, Imprimerie Nationale, 1851.

The efforts of our nearest continental neighbours have been particularly directed during the last nine years to the re-attainment of that rank and consideration which their nation formerly held among the naval powers of the world; and, admitting this to be a just and laudable policy for France to pursue, Great Britain should, at the same time, keep steadily in view the measures now being carried out in that country, conformably to the recommendation of the Commission of Inquiry just referred to, and must take corresponding measures to increase in due proportion the power, efficiency, and numerical strength of her naval forces, in order to maintain her present position. Thus, the naval arsenals of two great nations in alliance with each other, one of them impelled by a necessity of the first and highest order — that of providing effectually for its own security, are resounding with the din of warlike preparations, while both nations might be participating in the financial advantages and social benefits of a sound, substantial, and lasting peace.

It may be proper to observe here, that the Commission of Inquiry, in its sitting of the 3rd February, 1851, decided, that the number of ships of the line which, by the Ordonnance of 1846, was limited to 40, should be increased to 45, and that each ship should be provided with steam power. This was the number adopted, but it appears from the discussion which took place on the occasion, that the proposition of M. Charner, one of the members of the Commission, to increase the number to 50 ships of the line was rather postponed than rejected. It was recommended to have the greatest number possible of ships of the line finished, afloat, and ready armed whenever they might be required. The reason for adopting the smaller number was, that 45 ships would be finished in less time, and thus the funds voted would be economised, and the country be better prepared in the event of war soon breaking out. The number of ships actually finished is 47, and there is little doubt that it will soon amount to 50, as proposed by M. Charner.

In the sittings of the 12th February and the 10th March, 1851, it was resolved that the number of steam-frigates, *a grande vitesse*, should be 20, of frigates moved by sail and steam, also 20; at the same sitting it was decided that the number of corvettes should be fixed at 50, and that there should be 80 avisos. It was also decided that the construction of the 20 swift steam-frigates and the 50 corvettes should be completed gradually within the next ten years; at the same time it was determined that all sailing transports should be suppressed; and that, instead of them, there should be 20 steamers to serve as transports.[a] The line-of-battle steamers are recommended to be built on the model of the 'Napoléon,' formerly the 'Vingt-quatre-Fevrier;' the engines of this ship, though rated at 960 horse-power, can be worked up to 1500 horse-power, and the ship is capable of stowing coal for 10 days when steaming at full speed. It was subsequently resolved that the "Equipages de ligne" (ships' crews), and the "Mecaniciens," or engine-men, should continue to be kept up by means of the maritime conscription; that 14 ships of the line then afloat should undergo the alterations necessary to convert them into steam-ships; that the number should be made up to 30 from the ships

---

[a] The transport, 'Calvados,' which was lately launched at L'Orient, the first of twenty vessels of the same class, is said to have accommodation for 2500 men, 150 horses, and 1200 tons of stores.

then on the stocks, and that 20 of them should be completed within ten years.

In the decision respecting the establishment of ships' crews for manning the 45 ships of the line decreed by the Ordonnance of 1846, it was regulated that an adequate increase should be made in the number of companies, each of which was appointed to consist of 60 seamen of the first, second, and third classes, with 20 seamen apprentices; also that the establishment of seamen-gunners should be on so large a scale, that there might be one well-trained gunner to every gun in the ships to which they should be drafted.

The decisions of French Commissioners, on subjects referred to them, are not subject to change with a change of government, as with us; they are, on the contrary, immutable, and are perseveringly acted upon till they are effectually carried out. It is well known that the idea of constructing a great harbour at Cherbourg originated with Louis XIV., though the work was commenced only in the reign of Louis XVI. ; and, in the present year we have seen the completion of that vast work, which, in the language of the President of the Commission appointed in 1849, "is to contain the fleets which are to defend the French coasts and attack the English in their own country." [a]

Viewing France as that which she really is, a great power, whose safety depends upon her military forces, we have no right to cavil at any measures which the government of that country may adopt for its own

---

[a] In a speech delivered at a sitting of the Commission of Inquiry before referred to, Jan. 27th, 1851 (' Enquête Parlementaire,' tom. i., p. 149), M. Daru, after observing that, in the expedition to Rome, the whole French army was embarked and conveyed in ten days from Toulon to Civita Vecchia, infers that 24 steam frigates, 24 transports, 3 corvettes, and 3 avisos, concentrated at Dunkirk, Cherbourg, or Brest, would suffice to disembark 30,000 men and 3000 horses on any part of Great Britain or Ireland.

security against its powerful continental neighbours. Her military preponderance is as essential to her safety, as the maritime preponderance of Great Britain (an insular and colonial power) is indispensable to hers. Neither should be jealous nor distrustful of the other in any legitimate use which either may make of the powers with which nature has endowed them, respectively, for providing effectually for their own security.

The author makes these observations in no unfriendly spirit; he takes facts and circumstances as he finds them, and he uses them merely in proof of the necessity which Great Britain is under of taking corresponding measures to secure her own position, as a great maritime nation, among the powers of Europe. Sincerely disposed to value and maintain, in his humble sphere, the friendly relations which happily subsist between the governments of England and France, and relying on the assurances lately given by the head of the French nation, the author cannot but admire the policy by which the government of France is actuated in so reorganizing its maritime resources as to raise its navy to the highest possible degree of efficiency. Great Britain, as an insular and colonial empire, can maintain that high position in the rank of nations which she has gained by the instrumentality of her navy, only by keeping that noble branch of her service, not merely in a state barely sufficient to protect herself against any one maritime power, but fully adequate to defeat any maritime coalition to which political circumstances may at any future time give rise. And it must always be borne in mind, that, to enable the navy of Great Britain to act on equal terms with that of any continental nation, it ought by far to exceed the navy of such nation in the number of ships of war of like force.

Taking France, for example : while the naval power of that country will, in the event of a war, be chiefly collected in the two seas on the shores of which her great arsenals are established, that of our country must be dispersed over the whole world with strength sufficient, in every region, to protect her numerous colonies and widely-extended commerce. The fleets of England will, in time of war, have to blockade two great ports in the British Channel, instead of one, as in former wars, and must, moreover, have dominant power in all the waters which surround the British Isles.

The manning of the British navy was, in former times, so promptly accomplished by compulsory service, that, often, the dangers which menaced the country by sea were averted by a consciousness, on the part of the enemy, that our fleets were fully prepared to oppose any attempt at aggression. But now that the Government depends upon a voluntary enlistment for the supply of seamen to man our ships of war, there is always a risk of delays taking place when a fleet is to be fitted for service ; it will signify little that we have abundance of ships and of the *matériel* for arming them, if the brave men who are to serve in them are not forthcoming at the time of need. The French have still their law of compulsory enrolment, from which they form their ships' companies ; but Great Britain has only the inducement which a liberal bounty and a careful attention to comfort on board the ships offer, to enable her to procure the men who are to defend the country and maintain the glory of her arms in naval warfare.

A brief notice of naval tactics under sail will be given in the present work, because it will be long before sails can be entirely superseded by steam-engines, if this supercession should ever take place.

Steam fleets will be compelled occasionally, from exhaustion of fuel or from derangements of the steam machinery, to have recourse to sails ; and it is evident, therefore, that tactics with sails must not be hastily disregarded. A tract on naval warfare with steam is, however, indispensable at the present time, since evolutions which cannot be executed with precision and certainty, or even cannot be executed at all, with the sail, may be effectually accomplished by the steam machinery, while new evolutions and new formations must be subjects of contemplation ; and thus it is imperative that our seamen should render themselves equally expert in both systems. Before entering, however, upon the subject of naval tactics with steam, it will be proper to devote a section to the purpose of giving a brief history of the introduction of steam as a moving power to ships, and a brief notice of the nature and action of steam-machinery in its application to the *paddle* and the *screw*, together with an inquiry into the relative values of these agents, with respect to their powers of communicating motion, and to their conveniences in the armament of ships of war.

Aug. 16, 1858.

CONTENTS.

b

NAVAL WARFARE WITH STEAM.

SECTION I.

ON THE APPLICATION OF STEAM POWER TO SHIPS OF WAR.

1. It would be foreign to the plan of this work to enter into details respecting the invention of the steam-engine, or to describe the gradual improvements which it has subsequently undergone;[a] a brief notice only will be given of the several steps by which it has been rendered applicable to the purposes of navigation.[b]

In the beginning of the eighteenth century the Steam-Engine, or, as it was then called, the Atmospherical Engine, produced its effect solely by the admission of steam into the cylinder at its lower extremity; the steam by its elasticity forced the piston to the upper part of the cylinder, when, a vacuum being caused by a sudden condensation of the steam in consequence of a jet of cold water being introduced, the pressure of the atmosphere on the upper surface of the piston caused this to descend : steam being again admitted below, the piston was forced upwards; and, again, a vacuum being formed as before, the atmosphere caused the piston a second time to descend. This alternate ascent and descent of the piston caused corresponding movements of the pump-rod, by which means water was raised. The steam-engine was long employed for this purpose only.

---

[a] For a full explanation of the marine steam-engine in its present improved state, the reader is referred to the treatise on that important subject by Mr. Thomas J. Main, Mathematical Professor in the Royal Naval College, Portsmouth.

[b] The author wishes it to be understood that this historical and descriptive notice relating to steam is introduced only for the benefit of the general reader, or of those officers who may not have had the advantage of studying the subject at the Royal Naval College.

B

2. The first improvement by Watt consisted in admitting the steam alternately at the bottom and top of the cylinder, so that, when the vacuum was formed below the piston, the pressure of the steam above caused the piston to descend; and the vacuum being then formed above the piston, the pressure of the steam below caused it to ascend. In this manner a reciprocating motion of the piston was maintained; and, as the pressure of the steam could be made to exceed that of the atmosphere, a greater degree of power was obtained; and this augmented power was enabled to act uniformly on the piston. The patent for this great improvement was obtained by Mr. Watt in 1769; and, in 1780, Pickard took out one for converting the reciprocating motion of the pump-rod into a rotatory motion. This was effected simply by means of a crank, and in the following year Mr. Watt invented what he called the sun and planet wheel-work, by which the same end was gained as by the crank; and this rotatory motion was a great step towards the employment of the steam-engine as a means of propelling ships on the water. At length, in 1802, the first boat with paddle-wheels propelled by steam was constructed.

3. It would be improper to dwell on the supposed project of a Spanish captain named Garay, who is said, in 1543, to have exhibited a vessel propelled by poles to which motion was communicated by boiling water, or on the unsuccessful experiments made in France in 1774-5, and in America in 1783, to give motion to a vessel furnished with paddle-wheels, which were made to revolve by means of a small steam-engine; but it deserves to be particularly mentioned that in the years 1788-9 experiments were made at Dalswinton in Scotland on the use of paddle-wheels, at first moved by mechanical means, for the propulsion of vessels on water. These were commenced by a Mr. Millar of that place, and were conducted under his auspices by Messrs. Taylor and Symington; and to the former of these two engineers is ascribed the idea of employing steam-power to give motion to the wheels, which was

afterwards put in practice by the latter. Mr. Symington's experiments were carried on under the patronage
of Lord Thomas Dundas; and, in 1789, a boat called
the 'Charlotte Dundas,' propelled by a double stroke
engine (Watt's patent) and paddle-wheels, was tried
upon some water in the neighbourhood of Dalswinton;
it is said to have been moved at the rate of 5 miles in
an hour. Experiments of the same nature continued
to be made by the abovenamed gentlemen; and, in
1802, Symington built two steamboats which conveyed goods on the Forth and Clyde canals.

4. The American Chancellor Livingstone had, in
1798, made an unsuccessful attempt to construct a steamboat, to be used on the Hudson; and, in 1803, being in
France, he constructed a steam-vessel, in conjunction
with Fulton, to be used on the Seine: this also failed,
but Fulton afterwards visiting England, was introduced
to Symington, and was, by that engineer, allowed to
inspect the vessels which he had constructed. Fulton
subsequently returned to America; and, in 1807, he
completed a vessel with paddle-wheels, moved by a
steam-engine which had been executed by Boulton and
Watt in England: this vessel, called the 'Clermont,'
was the first which was employed as a passage-boat,
and its first voyage was made on the Hudson, from
New York to Albany.

5. The first steamboat which plied on the Thames is
said to have been brought from the Clyde by a Mr.
Dawson in 1813: as a speculation the measure failed;
but, from the year 1815, steam-vessels have constantly
been employed for the conveyance of passengers up
and down the river.

6. A Mr. Stevens, junior, of New York, is said to
have been the first who took a steamboat to sea; this
was about the year 1804, and the vessel is said to have
been moved by a machine resembling a smoke-jack: this
may consequently be considered as the first application
of the Screw Propeller in navigation. The first ship
propelled by steam which crossed the Atlantic was the
'Savannah,' a vessel of 350 tons burthen. It was built

and equipped at New York, and, in 1819, it proceeded
direct to Liverpool; from thence it proceeded to St.
Petersburg, and subsequently recrossed the Atlantic,
having used steam during the whole voyage. Between
the years 1842 and 1845 Her Majesty's steam sloop
'Driver,' commanded by Captains Harmer and Hayes,
made the circuit of the earth.

7. It may be interesting to know that as long since
as the year 1785 Mr. Bramah obtained a patent for a
submerged propeller on the principle, it is said, of a
windmill-sail; subsequently patents were obtained by
other persons for propellers constructed on similar
principles, which being moved by mechanical means,
sufficiently demonstrated the efficiency of that construction. In 1836, Captain Erecsson, a native of Sweden,
obtained a patent in England for a screw-propeller, and
a steam-vessel constructed by that engineer with the
screw at the stern was tried on the Thames, in presence
of the First Lord of the Admiralty and the Surveyor
General of the Navy; the success is said to have been
complete, but the new machine failed to gain the
approbation of the British Government. The subject
being, however, brought to the notice of Captain
Stockton, of the United States' Navy, then in London,
this officer strongly recommended it to the authorities
in America. Under his direction an iron vessel with
a screw propeller was constructed in England; and,
after crossing the Atlantic, it was employed on the
Delaware and Rariton Canal. This vessel afforded the
first practical evidence of the success of the screw as a
means of propulsion, both for the inland waters of a
country and on the high seas.

8. The greatest improvement which has been made in
the manner of applying steam as a moving power, with
respect to the union of force with economy, has consisted in what is called the expansive principle. It is
at present the custom to allow steam whose force of
elasticity is expressed by a pressure varying from 25 lbs.
to 40 lbs. per square inch, including the pressure of the
atmosphere, to enter the cylinder of a steam-engine;

and when the piston has moved through a space varying from two-fifths to three-fifths of the whole stroke
or range of the piston, to close the steam-slide so that
no more steam may enter till the piston is at the end of
the stroke, leaving that which has been admitted to
complete the stroke by its expansive power.

9. Now, if steam of a given elasticity be allowed to
act uniformly on the surface of the piston through the
whole length of the stroke, the efficient momentum of
the steam would be expressed by $p\,a\,l$; p denoting the
pressure of the steam on a square inch of the surface of
the piston, a the area of that surface in square inches,
and l the length of the stroke also in inches.   But if
the steam be cut off after the piston has moved through
a part of the stroke which is expressed by $m\,l$ (m being
a proper fraction), the efficient momentum of the ex-
panded steam during the remainder of the piston's
movement will be expressed by the integral of $\dfrac{a\,p\,m\,l\,d\,x}{x}$
between the limits $x = m\,l$ and $x = l$: (the density, elasticity, or pressure of the steam in any part of the
cylinder being inversely proportional to the space, or
distance of the piston from its place at the time the
steam was cut off.)   This integral is $a\,p\,m\,l$ hyp. log. $\dfrac{1}{m}$,
which added to $a\,p\,m\,l$, the momentum of the steam previously to being cut off, the sum is the efficient momentum of the steam thus acting expansively.   If $m = \frac{2}{15}$,
the hyp. log. of $\dfrac{1}{m}$ is equal (nearly) to 2 ; and the
whole momentum becomes $\frac{1}{3}\,a\,p\,l$ nearly.   Thus, with
$\frac{2}{15}$ths, or less than one-seventh, of the quantity of
steam, consequently of the quantity of fuel,[a] a power is
obtained equal to one-third of that produced by the
whole of the steam if allowed to act unexpansively ; it

---

[a] Since the pressure on a piston varies with the weight or density of the
steam, and the weight of a body of steam is equal to the weight of the water
which generates it, it follows that if the quantity of fuel consumed when the
steam is employed unexpansively be represented by 1, the quantity consumed
will be expressed by $\frac{1}{7}$ when the steam is used expansively.

follows also that, with steam to be used expansively, whose elastic force is 2½ times as great as that of steam used unexpansively, if it be cut off when the piston has moved two-fifteenths of the whole length of stroke, the effective momentum will be the same as that which would be produced by the steam of less elasticity when used unexpansively : while the consumption of steam, and therefore of fuel, in the former case is only one-third (= 2½ × $\frac{2}{15}$) of the consumption in the latter case. It must be observed, however, that, in order to resist a double expansive force of steam, the machinery ought to have a double strength, and would, consequently, be twice as heavy. In the above investigation no notice is taken of the effects of friction on the movement of the piston; this friction, and the imperfect vacuum in the cylinder, are causes of considerable loss of power in all steam-machinery.

10. Experience seems to show that these retarding forces may, together, be estimated at about one-fifth of the whole power of the steam; and there is a further diminution, when the steam acts expansively, on account of the loss of heat occasioned by the expansion of a gas ; and this, when the steam is allowed to expand to double its original volume, has been estimated at about one-twentieth of the whole power. It follows, as is observed by Messrs Seaward and Capel,[a] that there may come a time during a stroke when the power of the steam becomes less than the force of resistance against the piston, in which case the piston would stop if it were not for the momentum previously acquired. The same gentlemen observe that there must consequently, in practice, be a limit to the expansive principle ; and it is concluded that a cylinder having a 3 feet stroke, in which the steam is cut off at one-third of the range, would be nearly as efficient as a cylinder having a 6 feet stroke in which the steam is cut off at one-sixth, the consumption of fuel being equal. It is recommended that, for marine engines, the expansive

[a] Copy of Letter to the Hon. H. L. Corry, M.P., on the use of High Pressure Steam in the Steam-Vessels of the Royal Navy.   1846.

force of the steam should not exceed 10 or 12 lbs. per square inch above the pressure of the atmosphere ; and Messrs. Seaward and Co. propose that, for engines of great power, the steam should be cut off at one half or three-fifths of the stroke.

11. Marine engines of the present day are said to be from 20 to 50 per cent. more powerful in giving motion to ships than those of former times ; this greater speed, and the diminished consumption of fuel, are due to the adoption of the *wave principle* in forming the bows of ships, the improved construction of machinery, and the employment of more elastic steam.

12. The only means of propelling ships by the agency of steam which have as yet been brought to the test of experiment, and which have been generally adopted, are the Paddle-Wheel and the Screw ; but both of these, in their forms, have been variously modified.

13. The reciprocating motion of the piston rods in the two steam cylinders of the engine being made to act, by means of cranks, on the shaft or common axle of the paddle-wheels, causes these to take a revolving motion about that axle ; and the reaction of the water against the floats or paddle-boards as they revolve, impels the vessel forward.

14. When the paddle-boards are permanently fixed, as they usually are, in planes passing through the shaft, they necessarily enter the water obliquely ; and it is only when any one board is in a vertical position, under the shaft, that the reaction of the water against it is direct. In other positions the boards press against the water in directions oblique to the line of the vessel's motion : on entering the water the boards exert a pressure downwards, while in emerging they lift up a body of water, and both these actions cause violent strains and vibrations in the vessel.

15. The *Dip*, or the immersion of the lowest paddle-board in the water, should in general be equal to the breadth of the board, so that the upper edge may be *a-wash*, or on a level with the surface of the water. If the dip should be less than this, part of the engine's

power would be ineffective in producing the motion of
the ship; if greater, part of that power would be spent
in overcoming the greater resistance experienced in
alternately depressing and raising the water about the
entering and emerging boards.

16. The diameters of paddle-wheels should not exceed
four and a half times the length of stroke, for this
reason, that if more, the " slip " [a] of the paddle will be
great. With a wheel of such proportion the " slip "
would be about 20 per cent. The inner edge of the
paddle-board should have as nearly as possible the speed
of the ship : the slip will then be at a minimum.

17. The length of a paddle-board should be about, or
rather more than $\frac{1}{3}$ the diameter of the wheel. When
the diameters of the wheels exceed $4\frac{1}{2}$ times the length
of stroke, the engines ordinarily constructed are not
capable of driving them effectively, so that the power of
the engine is not fully developed. This power should
correspond to the velocity assigned to the piston, suppose
200 or 220 feet per minute ; and, to be enabled to obtain
this with a larger wheel the paddle-board must be nar-
rowed, which would augment the slip, and under adverse
circumstances this might become very considerable.

18. These are the proportions for sea-going vessels,
and the whole power of the engine should be effective
when the vessel is at the mean draught of water, viz.
the mean between her extreme light, and load-lines.
In river vessels, perhaps, a diameter of wheel equal to
about four times the length of stroke would be a good
proportion. It is evident that the paddle-boards of
sea-going vessels should be more deeply immersed than
those of vessels which navigate a river, since at sea, on
account of the vessel's pitches, the boards are great part
of the time out of water.

19. From the known dimensions of the paddle-wheels
in several vessels of war, it appears that the diameters
of the wheels vary nearly with the square root of the

---

[a] Loss of power caused by the recession of the water *aftward* from the
paddle-boards.

horse-power of the engine ; and, with a vessel whose engine has a power equal to 200 horses, the diameter of the wheel, between the outer extremities of the paddle-boards, is about 20 feet ; the lengths of the paddles are rather less than half, and the breadths between one-ninth and one-tenth of the diameter. Hence, if the circumference of a wheel 20 feet in diameter be furnished with 20 paddle-boards 2 feet broad, when the upper edge of the lowest vertical board is a-wash, there will be three boards wholly or partly immersed, one will be nearly entering the surface of the water, and a fifth will have just emerged from it.

20. If a vessel be retained at rest in still water while the wheels revolve, the reaction of the water against a paddle-board will be the greatest when the board is in a vertical position in the water, but this will not always be the case when the vessel is free to move by the rotation of the wheel. In order to explain this subject, let S be the centre of the wheel's rotation, and A B the momentary position of a paddle making, with the vertical line S Z, an angle Z S B represented by θ. Let V be the velocity of the point C (supposed to be the centre of pressure on A B) in a direction perpendicular to the surface of the paddle A B, and V′ the velocity of the vessel in the water, in a horizontal direction; then, by the Resolution of Forces or Velocities, V cos. θ is that velocity in a direction perpendicular to the surface of the paddle A B; therefore V − V′ cos. θ will express the relative velocity of the paddle and vessel in the same direction. But the resistance of a fluid against a body moving in it varies with the square of the velocity ;[a] therefore $(V − V′ \cos. \theta)^2$ may denote the force of resistance, or pressure, against the paddle : this being multiplied by V, the product is the efficient

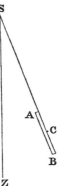

Fig. 1.

---

[a] Experiments have shown that this rule is very nearly correct notwithstanding the perturbation of the water by the wheel's rotation.

momentum of that resistance in a direction perpendicular to the surface of the paddle ; and consequently

$$(V - V' \cos. \theta)^2 \, V \cos. \theta$$

is the efficient force by which that resistance impels the vessel forward horizontally : which, for the vertical paddle, where $\theta = 0$, becomes

$$(V - V')^2 \, V.$$

21. But in these expressions it is supposed that the paddles are wholly immersed : this is evidently not the case with the oblique paddles when the upper edge of the lowest vertical paddle is on a level with the surface of the water, for then the immersed part of an oblique paddle is expressed by $S B - S A \sec. \theta$; or, r being the radius of the wheel to the outer extremity of a paddle-board, and a the difference between r and the breadth (b) of the paddle, it is expressed by $r - a \sec. \theta$: consequently the ratio between the efficient resistances against a vertical and an oblique paddle will be as

$$(V - V')^2 b \, V \; : \; (V - V' \cos. \theta)^2 \, V \, (r \cos. \theta - a).$$

These expressions being put in numbers according to the data, for different values of θ, it will be found that the first will be less than the second till the part of the paddle's breadth which is out of the water causes a diminution of power which more than compensates for the superiority which is due to the obliquity.

Making the differential of this last expression equal to zero, we may obtain the value of θ which makes the resistance a maximum. Assuming $V' = \frac{4}{5} V, r = 10$ feet, $a = 8$ feet, whence $b = 2$ feet, the greatest resistance takes place when $\theta = 18°$; and the force on the vertical paddle is, to that on the oblique paddle in this position, as 10 to 10·865.

The resistance against a vertical paddle being thus proved to be less than the resistance against an oblique paddle, in the most effective part of the motion of the latter, it follows that to obtain equal speed for two vessels, one of which is furnished with paddles of the ordinary kind, and the other with such as are kept by machinery always in a vertical position, the wheels being of equal dimensions, that which has the vertical paddles must revolve with greater velocity than the other, and consequently it must cause a greater consumption of steam and fuel.

22. If a vessel were at rest, every point in the arms or radii of a paddle-wheel would, during a revolution, describe a circle; but when the vessel is in motion, each point describes a trochoidal curve, which is the common cycloid when the forward rectilinear motion of the vessel, during the time of a revolution of the wheel, is equal to the circumference of the circle which would be described by the point if the vessel were at rest. Every point farther from the centre of the wheel than that which describes a common cycloid must describe what is called a curtate or contracted cycloid, and every point nearer the centre a prolate or extended cycloid.

23. The curves described by points on the opposite edges of a paddle-board, and the various positions assumed by a paddle-board during a revolution of the wheel, are exhibited in the annexed figure:—

Fig. 2.

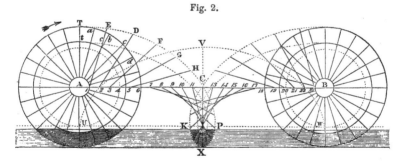

Let A be the centre of a wheel having twenty-four paddle-boards, and let T be a point on the exterior edge of one of the boards when in a vertical position; also, let the wheel turn about A in the direction T *a b c*, &c., and, at the same time, let the centre A be carried towards B by the movement of the vessel, the straight line, A B, being supposed equal to the circumference of the circle, described about A by some point as U, if the vessel were at rest. Then, if A B be divided into twenty-four equal parts in the points 1, 2, 3, &c., the board at T will take, successively, the positions indicated by 1 E, 2 D, 3 F, &c.; and when it coincides in direction with A C, the centre, A, being then at 6, the wheel will have performed one-quarter of a revolution, the outer edge of the board having described the cycloidal curve T E . . . C, and the inner edge the curve t e . . . 11. The vessel continuing its rectilinear motion and the wheel its revolution, the edges of the board will describe the looped curves at C P X shown in the figure; and when A has arrived at C, half a revolution of the wheel being performed, the board T will have the vertical position C X. The curves described by the points T and t during the second half of the revolution of the wheel will be symmetrical with those described during the first half; and the whole revolution will be completed when A has arrived at the point B. If P K represent the surface of the water, the oblique lines within the space P X K will show the positions of the several paddle-boards while in the water.

The position of the point U may be found on dividing the velocity of the vessel, in feet per hour, by the number of revolutions of the wheel per hour (or by the number of double strokes made by the piston of the engine per hour); the quotient is the circumference, in feet, of the circle whose radius is A U; from this value of the circumference the radius A U may be obtained. A circle whose circumference is thus determined is called the circle of rotation. In vessels having the ordinary speed, the radius of the circle of rotation is equal to about two-thirds of the radius of the wheel, to the outer edges of the paddle-boards.

The centre of pressure in any revolving plane is that in which, if the whole pressure were concentrated, the effect would be equal to that which takes place when the pressure is uniformly distributed over the plane. In a paddle-board the position of this centre varies with the depth of its immersion; and if, as an approximation to its position, its distance from the centre of the wheel be considered as equal to $r - \frac{1}{3} b$, representing this value by r', the expression

$$(V - V' \cos. \theta) V (r \cos. \theta - a) r' d \theta$$

being integrated between the limits of θ, the result would give the whole pressure on the wheel, and be the equivalent to the power of the engine. It is at present the practice to measure the effective power of a marine engine by means of the *Indicator* and *Dynamometer*.

24. If a spiral line were traced on the convex surface of a cylinder, so as to coincide with the hypotenuse of a right-angled triangle wound about it, the base of the triangle being equal to the circumference of the cylinder, and disposed in a plane perpendicular to the axis, then, if through every point in the spiral line straight lines are drawn perpendicular to the axis of the cylinder, those lines will be in the superficies of what is called the blade or feather of a screw. If all these perpendiculars are of equal length, their outer extremities will form the periphery of the helix : the distance between two points on this periphery, measured parallel to the axis of the cylinder or screw, is called the *pitch* of the screw.

25. If a screw thus formed is attached to a floating body, as a ship, with its axis in a horizontal position, and the screw is made, by means of machinery connected with a steam-engine, to revolve on that axis in the water, the pressure exerted by one surface of the blade on the water will be accompanied by a reaction of the water against that surface ; and the force of this reaction, resolved in a direction parallel to the axis of the screw, will cause the ship to move in that direction. The reaction of the water against any point on the blade will depend on the velocity of the screw's rotation, on the depth of the point below the surface of the water, and on various other circumstances.

26. If the water, pressed by the posterior surfaces of the float-boards of a paddle-wheel, or by the posterior surface of the blade of a screw, could remain stationary so as to form a perfect fulcrum, the whole force of its

reaction would be effective in propelling the ship; but
this is not the case—the water pressed by the paddle or
blade recedes *aftward*, and therefore the reaction of the
water is that only which is due to the difference between
the velocity of rotation in the paddle or screw and that
of the water's recession.

It should be observed that the action of the water on
the anterior surface of a paddle, or on the anterior surface of a screw-blade, is also a cause of retardation in a
ship's motion.

If the pitch of a screw were 10 feet, one revolution
of the screw would, if it were not for these impediments,
cause the ship to be moved forward 10 feet; whereas, in
ordinary circumstances, it is moved only about 8 feet.[a]

27. In the early days of screw-propulsion the propelling surface consisted of a single and continuous blade
or feather, making at least one entire revolution about
the spindle or axis of the screw; but this formation was
soon found to be defective in practice, on account, first,
of the great cross-strain it gave to one side of the axis,
and the disturbance it occasioned in the different parts
of the system; secondly, the severe vibratory motion it
caused in the stern, which is the weakest part of the
vessel.   It was at first supposed that all parts of the

---

[a] Tᴀʙʟᴇ I.—Showing the elements of several vessels.

Name of the Vessel.	Horses' Power.	Diameter of Wheel, in feet.	Number of Strokes of Engine.	Speed observed in miles, per hour.	Diameter to centre of Pressure, in feet.	Speed of ditto, in miles per hour.	Loss by Slip, &c.
Messenger .	200	19·33	20½	9·75	17·65	12·92	3·17
Salamander.	220	20·33	15	8·15	18·36	9·83	1·68
Phœnix . .	220	20·33	21	11·70	18·57	13·92	2·22
Monarch. .	200	21·00	20½	10·72	19·31	14·13	3·41
Hermes . .	140	17·50	18	6·30	15·86	10·19	3·89
Firebrand .	140	17·00	24	10·15	15·38	13·18	3·03
Fire-fly . .	140	17·50	20	8·30	15·81	11·29	2·99
Magnet . .	140	16·00	29½	9·15	11·77	12·39	3·24
			means	9·03		12·23	3·20

---

*It therefore appears that the average loss by slip is about one-third of the
whole effective speed : the ratio of the loss to the whole speed varies very sensibly
for the several vessels considered individually ; but, in general, we believe that
one-third will be very near the truth.*

surface of a screw are equally effective in producing
propulsion, and this opinion led to the formation of
a screw having an entire, or more than one, convolution
about the axis; but the supposition is erroneous, and
so much the more as the screw revolves on its axis with
greater velocity.

28. The most effective part of a screw-blade is that
which is near the periphery of the spiral, and the action
of any part on the water becomes less as the part is
nearer the axis or spindle. Science has, however, as yet
done little in investigating the propelling properties of a
screw in water; and the intricacy of the subject is such
that the formulæ expressing those properties are too
complex to admit of being practically applicable except
under very limited conditions.

29. If the screw were supposed to consist of a feather
or blade forming two or three convolutions in the length
of the axis, the reaction of the water on it would be
precisely the same as on a screw with one convolution
only in its length, since corresponding parts in each of
the two or three portions are in corresponding positions
in the water, and all are in action at the same time.
The water between the posterior part of one turn of the
blade and the anterior part of the next, towards the
stern of the ship, is nearly quiescent, the water at
the posterior surface of the last turn of the blade alone
receding; and there appears to be no foundation for
the opinion that the water between every two turns of
the blade is made to revolve with the screw, or even to
be in any state of commotion.

30. Experiment soon showed that, when the length
of the screw was diminished so that the feather had
successively three-quarters, one-half, and even less
than one-third of a turn in the length, there did not
appear, with equal engine-power, to be any diminution
in the speed of the ship. This apparently anomalous
circumstance caused at first much surprise, and the
cause of it is not, even now, free from uncertainty;
but the explanation, for which the author is indebted to
Mr. Lloyd, Director-General of the Steam Department

at the Admiralty, is the most satisfactory that has yet
been offered. This gentleman supposes a screw, whose
blade makes one complete turn only in the length, to be
divided by planes all perpendicular to the axis of the
screw, and at small intervals from one another, so that
the surface of the screw is divided into a great number
of sectoral or fan-like areas oblique to the axis, and
following one another in succession from one end of the
screw to the other. Now, the water in which the screw
turns being supposed at rest, a vertical lamina of water,
which is acted upon by the first of these sectors, is, by
the pressure of the posterior surface in the revolution
of the screw, pressed with a certain force towards the
after-part of the screw ; the water thus receding is
acted upon by the second sectoral portion of the screw
in its revolution, and impelled *aftward*, but with less
force than before, on account of the retiring movement
of the water : a part of this water is acted upon by the
third sectoral portion of the screw in its revolution, and
still impelled *aft*, but with a force further diminished by
the greater retiring movement of the water, and so on,
to the end of the screw.

31. Thus, the pressive force of the screw on the water,
and, consequently, the reaction of the water, by which
the ship is propelled forward, go on diminishing ; and
the *slip*, or recession of the water, goes on increasing
with the length of the screw. The diminution of the
power of motion on this account is probably very small
when the velocity of the screw's rotation is small ; and,
in that case, an entire screw with one turn in its length
may have some advantages ; but, when the velocity of
rotation is great, it is probable that the propelling power
of the *after*-part of the screw becomes so small as to
permit its removal without diminishing in a sensible
degree the speed of the ship ; in fact, experience has
shown that, with high velocities of rotation, one-third
or one-fourth of an entire convolution of the blade is
sufficient to produce the full effect of the moving
power.

32. In what has been said it is supposed that the water

has immediate access to the screw, and that the particles pressed by it are free to move *aftward*; but neither of these suppositions is correct. From the position of the screw, in an aperture close under the ship's counter, the water, which is divided by the body of the ship, subsequently flows obliquely towards the screw; and, again, the water, after being pressed by the screw, is broken by the stern-post and rudder, where, being arrested, part of it is forced forward in the direction of the ship's motion: on both these accounts the power of the screw must be in some degree modified; in some cases, indeed, the *slip* has been found to be negative, that is, the actual speed of the ship has been greater than the theoretical speed, or that which is due to the power of the engine.

33. From such considerations, and from repeated experiments, it has been determined that the best form which can be given to a screw is that of two halves of a spiral feather, placed on opposite sides of the axle of the screw in reverse positions: these, while they occupy only half the space in length which they would otherwise require, are found, with equal surface, more efficient than the continuous spiral formerly in use.

The two sectors, or fan-shaped blades, composing the present screw, have generally what is called a uniform pitch; that is, they constitute two equal and similar figures, one on each side of a plane perpendicular to the axle and bisecting the length or pitch of the original screw, supposed to be of one complete turn: each blade occupying exactly half that length. But some screws have been made which occupy much less of the length, and with what is called an *increasing* pitch: thus, imagining a vertical plane perpendicular to the axle to divide the whole pitch in the ratio of 11 to 12, the forward fan occupies half the shorter portion and the aftward fan half the longer portion; consequently, the extent of the interval between the extremities of the two blades, if measured on a line parallel to the axle, is half the entire pitch of the complete screw. This is Mr. Wood-

croft's construction : in that of Mr. Atherton the two
fans are equal and similar to one another, but each is
formed so that the parts about the axle are portions of
spirals, of smaller pitch than those of the parts about
the extremities, the pitch increasing gradually from the
axle towards the periphery.

34. In a manner similar to that which has been used in
finding the propulsive effect of water on a common
paddle-wheel, may be found the effect of water on the
blades of a screw in giving motion to a vessel. Thus,
let C D be a horizontal
line parallel to the keel
of the ship or to the
screw-axle, and let Z C
be at right angles to it in
a plane passing through
C D, perpendicular to the
radius or arm of a screw
blade ; also let A B in the
same plane be the inter-
section of the plane with
the anterior surface of the
blade. Imagine A B at
present to be a straight
line ; and let it be ob-
served that the vertical plane in which any point, as
C, in A B revolves about the screw-axle is perpendicular to that axle, and to the horizontal line C D.

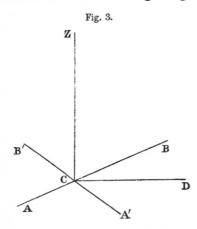

Fig. 3.

Now, let the velocity of the point C, by the revolution of the screw-blades about the screw-axle, be represented by V, and be supposed to act in the direction
Z C ; and let the horizontal velocity of C, by the forward movement of the vessel, be represented by V', in
the direction C D ; also let the angle Z C B $= \theta$: then
Z C D being a right angle, V' cos. θ is the velocity of
the ship resolved perpendicularly to A B, and V sin. θ
is the velocity of the blade also resolved perpendicularly to A B ; consequently V sin. $\theta -$ V' cos. θ represents the relative velocity of the paddle and ship in the

same direction. It follows that $(V \sin. \theta - V' \cos. \theta)^2$
$V \cos. \theta$ expresses the efficient momentum of the water,
in the horizontal direction, in propelling the vessel.
Representing V' by $n V$, the expression becomes

$$V^2 (\sin. \theta - n \cos. \theta)^2 \cos. \theta,$$

and this quantity is to be a maximum.

Making its differential equal to zero, and reducing,
we have

$$\tan. \theta = \frac{3 n}{2} \pm \tfrac{1}{2} (9 n^2 + 8)^{\frac{1}{4}}.$$

Assuming $V' = \tfrac{1}{2} V$, or $n = \tfrac{1}{2}$, we have $\theta = 67° 57'$ or
$139° 27'$.

When the angle Z C B $(= \theta)$ is $67° 57'$, the motion
of A B, resolved vertically, is upwards, or towards
Z; in the other case the blade has the position
A′ C B′, and its motion is downwards. If n were
diminished, the first value of θ would become less : now
the velocity of a point, as C, on the blade being
greater as it is farther from the screw-axle, the value of
n being then less, the value of the angle Z C B would
be diminished ; which shows that A B, instead of being
a straight line, should be a curve such that a tangent
to it at any point should make a smaller angle with a
line perpendicular to the radius of the blade, than is
made by a tangent at a point nearer the screw-axle.

35. A propeller, whether it be a wheel or a screw,
should be so constructed and applied as, by its action,
to disturb the water as little as possible in directions
which do not tend to propulsion. This condition, as
already observed, Art. 14, is very imperfectly fulfilled
in the common radiating paddle-wheel, the boards of
which being fixed in the direction of radii, press the
water down in entering, and raise it in emerging. A
considerable portion of the force of the engine is thus
absorbed, and there is formed a negative wave, which
is attended with a vibration of the vessel.

36. These defects have been somewhat obviated by
an invention which was patented by Mr. Galloway in

1829, by which the paddle-boards are made to turn or
feather, so as to enter, pass through, and emerge from
the water in positions the most advantageous for propelling a vessel with less of the vibration and loss of
power which arise from the action of the radiating
paddles.   The machinery on each side of the vessel
consists of two wheels, both of which are affixed to the
main axle, but are not concentric, and the feathering
motion of the board is produced by affixing a short arm
to one face of each paddle-board at an angle of 120
degrees with its plane, the boards turning on horizontal
axles, which pass through the extremities of the radii
of one of the two excentric wheels.   A rod is connected
at one end, by a joint, with the extremity of that short
arm, and at the opposite end, also by a joint, with the
excentric part of the axle.   By the revolution of the
double wheel the rod makes a constantly varying angle
with the short arm which is attached to the paddle
board, and this causes a corresponding variation in the
angle which the paddle-board makes with the radii of
the wheel, so that by a due adjustment of the length of
the rod the board is made to enter and leave the water
at an angle of about 30 degrees with a vertical line,
this being the angle at which, in general, the reaction
of the water against the board is the most favourable
for propelling the vessel.

37. This improvement has tended greatly to increase
the speed of paddle steamers, and the best sea-going
vessels are now fitted with feathering paddles.   Such
paddles have been applied to her Majesty's yacht, 'Vic-
toria and Albert,' and others; and they are particularly
applicable to that description of vessel, as well as to
packets, which are employed in short passages, and in
which the load line, or draught of water, does not
much vary; but for vessels employed on foreign
voyages, and particularly for ships of war employed
on cruising services, which are necessarily of considerable duration, they are not convenient : vessels so employed being at first deeply laden, and subsequently
much lightened, it would become necessary to have

recourse to the difficult and scarcely practicable operation of *reefing* the paddles.[a]

When paddles are deeply immersed, as in vessels heavily laden, their action is materially impeded, and a great part of the power of the engine uselessly absorbed. On the other hand, when vessels are too lightly laden, the paddle-boards do not take sufficient hold of the water, and the slip is consequently greatly increased. In the former case, when the greatest effort is required to be made to overcome the increased amount of resistance to the motion of the ship, the effect of the paddle is impeded by the greater body of water which it has to lift up in rising through the water, and hence the numerous contrivances for reefing paddles. To these evils must be added that which arises, when there is much swell, from the rolling of the vessel; one paddle being too deeply immersed, and the other not sufficiently so, and sometimes not at all.

38. The injury done to the stern of a ship by the shake of the screw is a result much to be dreaded in a general use of that implement, whatever its advantages may be in other respects, and a sufficient number of experiments have not yet been made to ascertain the effects of long continued screw-propulsion at full speed. Such experiments should therefore be made and continued *à l'outrance* with all classes of vessels, more particularly steam-frigates, block-ships, and the first ships of the line fitted with screws. There are indications that the results may not be satisfactory, and, if so, it should be seen by what means this defect may be obviated. The screw is no doubt preferable to the paddle-wheel as a propelling implement; the defects now under notice arise only from its being placed in the dead wood, where it is subject to the cross strains it receives in passing through a body of water in a state of perturbation.

---

[a] In the trials of the 'Basilisk' and 'Niger' (Art. 54), the paddles of the former were reefed several times according as she became lighter; but this was found so inconvenient that she was ordered to retain them as fixed relatively with her mean immersion.

39. If the water reacted upon the screw of a steamer precisely as a nut reacts against the threads of a screw which works into it, the vessel would move through a space equal to the pitch of the screw in the time that the latter makes one revolution on its axis; but such speed is not realized in practice, first, on account of the recession of the water (the slip) from behind the screw, after being acted upon by the latter; secondly, the water in advance of the screw is not free to fill the void caused by the recession of the back-water, but arrives at the face of the screw in a disturbed state, in consequence of the displacement at the bows of the vessel, and the subsequent convergence towards the after part; thus producing cross actions and strains upon the blades of the screw, and forming an eddy round the stern of the ship, all of which affect considerably the propelling action of the screw. If the screw could be placed out of the vortices of this body of water, no doubt an important improvement would be made in screw propulsion.

40. Steam propulsion cannot be well combined with that of the wind in paddle-propelled vessels. In the first place the funnel prevents the use of the main-sail, as stated in the report of the trial between the ' Reynard ' and the ' Plumper.' Again, when the wind is *a-beam* in a breeze of considerable strength, the lee-paddle is too much, and the weather-paddle too little, immersed to be efficient; and in a strong breeze, a vessel will go faster before the wind with her sails alone, or with her steam alone, than with both combined. In fact the sails can scarcely be used unless the paddle-wheels are disconnected from the engine, and this process, as well as that of connecting them again, is very difficult. The expedient of removing some of the paddle-boards, and turning into the water that part of the wheel which is thus dismantled, is a tedious operation, and might be extremely detrimental in a war-steamer, which should ever be prepared to put forth all her power. The screw, on the contrary, may be disconnected with great facility at

any time, and consequently screw-propelled vessels may sail more and steam less than those furnished with paddles; their steam may thus be reserved for strong head winds or calms, and in emergencies incidental to the operations of war.

41. Feathering-paddles are particularly objectionable for ships of war, as they are even more likely to be damaged by shot than paddles of the common kind,[a] since shot has been known to pass between the spokes without disabling, or even touching, any part of the wheel, which could scarcely be the case if the boards were applied on the feathering principle.

42. Fixed paddle-boards, therefore, continue to be used in Her Majesty's service, but they are of improved form, for which a patent was granted to Mr. Field in 1833. The improvement consists in dividing the fixed board into several narrow slips, which are placed somewhat behind each other, with inclinations which correspond to the cycloidal curves they describe; these enter the water in immediate succession, and thus permit a great part of the water, which would otherwise be forced downwards in the descending movement, and upwards in the ascent of the boards, to escape through the spaces between them, while the slips overlapping each other in horizontal directions intercept and act upon all the horizontal filaments of the fluid, thus preventing a certain portion of the power of the engine from being wasted. The improved paddle-wheels generally used in the United States consist of a combination of two or more common paddle-wheels side by side, on each side of the vessel, and moving on the same shaft or axle, the paddle-boards being so placed that each is in a position between two boards of the collateral wheel. These wheels are of great magnitude, and being found very efficient in smooth water, are preferred to any of the expedients adopted in Europe to obviate the defects of the radiating paddles.—(Lardner, on the Steam-Engine, p. 496.)

---

[a] M'Kinnon's Steam Warfare, page 221.

43. Two instruments are now generally employed to determine the power of a Marine Steam-Engine; one of them shows the expansive power of the steam in the cylinder, and the other the force of impulsion in a screw-propelled vessel by the pressure on the screw shaft in the direction of its length. The first of these, called the *Indicator*, consists of a hollow cylinder of small dimensions, whose top is open, the lower end being fitted to be screwed on to the top or bottom of the engine-cylinder; a stop-cock at the bottom acts as a four-way cock, and admits either the external air or the steam; a piston works steam tight in the small cylinder, and a spiral spring is attached to the top of the piston, and to a fixed cross piece above it, so that this spring, which is contained in a tube affixed to the piston, acts against the power of steam which presses the piston up, and registers its force. The instrument being screwed on that part of the steam-cylinder from which the indication is required, and the stop-cock being opened, there is a communication between the interior of the steam-cylinder and that of the Indicator. Now if the Indicator be attached to the top of the steam-cylinder, and a vacuum exist above the piston of the latter, the piston of the indicator is, by the atmospherical pressure above it, forced to the bottom of the cylinder in which it moves; and when the steam from the boiler enters the top of the steam-cylinder, to force down its piston, the steam entering the lower part of the indicator-cylinder presses its piston upwards, this motion being retarded by the spiral spring already mentioned. To the top of the piston-tube in which the spring works, and at right angles to it, is affixed an arm, the extremity of which carries a pencil, which by the reciprocating motion of the piston-tube would describe on a plane surface at rest a straight line whose extremities would indicate the greatest or least elastic forces or pressures of the steam in the cylinder of the steam engine during each stroke of its piston, but would not show the pressure at any particular portion of the stroke.

When the indicator is not in communication with the cylinder of the steam engine, the piston in its cylinder is held in equilibrio by the equal pressures of the atmosphere above and below it.   In this state the spiral spring is at its greatest extension, and consequently does not press against the top of the piston. The point at which the pencil then stands on the straight line is marked zero, and is designated the atmospheric point.   The line being graduated, the divisions are numbered 1, 2, 3, &c., increasing upwards and downwards from the zero point; and when the indicator, being connected with the steam-cylinder of the engine, is in action, the numbers indicate, in pounds, the elastic pressure of the steam; the upward numbers denoting pounds above, and the lower, pounds below the pressure of the atmosphere ($= 14\cdot75$ lbs. on a square inch).

The pencil, however, instead of pressing against a plane surface, is made to press upon the convex surface of a cylindrical barrel which is turned by some part of the machinery on an axis parallel to the piston-rod; it consequently describes a curve of double curvature, the figure and ordinates of which indicate by inspection the varying elasticity of the steam in the cylinder of the engine.

44. The indicator should be applied both at the top and bottom of the steam cylinder, and a mean of its measures taken, as the values of the pressure above and below the piston are often different on account of differences in the lengths of the slides where the steam is introduced; also on account of the position of the crank at the time the steam is cut off.   The following are the general conclusions drawn from the nature of the line described by the pencil on the cylindrical surfaces against which it presses.

1. If the pencil describes a straight line upwards or downwards, the piston is not moving; but, in the first case, the steam pressure in the engine-cylinder is increasing, in the other case it is decreasing.

2. If the line is horizontal, proceeding to the right

or left hand, the steam pressure does not vary; but, in the first case, the piston is descending; in the second it is ascending.

3. If the line proceeds obliquely to the right upwards, or to the right downwards; in the first case the steam pressure is increasing and the piston is descending; in the other case, the pressure is decreasing and the piston descends.

4. If the line proceeds obliquely to the left downwards or to the left upwards; in the first case the pressure is decreasing and the piston ascends; in the other case, the pressure is increasing and the piston ascends.

45. The indicator may also be used for ascertaining particulars of some of the internal parts of the engine without actual inspection; for example, it may serve for the formation of the "slide diagram," in which the string that turns the barrel of the indicator is fixed to the cross-head of the slide, instead of that of the piston, and thus the index shows on paper the various positions of the slide. It will indicate if the slides are properly set, or leaky, if the steam ports are of the proper size, &c. &c. &c., for which the reader is referred to Mr. Main's interesting work on that subject.[a]

The scale of the indicator for high pressure (atmospheric) engines should be made to extend considerably above the atmospheric line, but it need not of course go below it.

When the Russian war steamer 'Wladimir' was tried in the Thames in 1848 the average pressure of steam on the piston by the indicator was $20 \cdot 275$ (-1 for friction) $= 19 \cdot 275$ in each of the two cylinders. Hence the surface of each piston being 4214 square inches,

---

[a] The reader will find a detailed account, illustrated by a good engraving, of this beautiful instrument in Mr. Main's treatise on the Marine Steam Engine already noticed, and which instrument, that distinguished author has well said, is, in the hands of a skilful engineer, to the steam engineer as the stethoscope of the physician; disclosing at any instant, and under any circumstances, the actual power of the engine, revealing the secret workings of the whole inner system, and detecting minute derangements in parts obscurely situated.

the length of stroke 6 feet, and the number of revolutions 19 per minute, the indicated horse power was for both engines 1122·38 : thus—

$$\frac{4214 \times 19 \cdot 275 \times 6 \times 38}{33000} = 561 \cdot 19. \quad \text{One engine;}$$

Consequently—

$$561 \cdot 19 \times 2 = 1122 \cdot 38 \text{ for the two engines.}^{a}$$

46. The second instrument above alluded to is called a Dynamometer : when employed to measure the pressure on a screw-shaft, it shows the power of the engine to propel the ship ; and this object is obtained by means of a lever, simple or compound.

In the revolution of the screw the reaction of the water against its surface, supposed to be resolved in the direction of the shaft or axle, produces a pressure in that direction and, consequently, propels the ship ; and its intensity is a measure of the power of the steam engine. The end of the screw-shaft presses, through the intervention of a pin, against a *knife edge,* on a lever, which it may be sufficient to consider as simple ; this lever is in a vertical position, with its lower extremity fixed by a joint, as a fulcrum, to an immoveable object (the *plomer block*) in the ship. The opposite end of the lever is connected, by a joint, with one end of a rod in a horizontal position, the opposite end being

---

^a The following empirical formula is given by Mr. Roughton for calculating, with a near approximation to the truth, the speed of paddle-wheel steamers, one of the data being obtained from the Indicator :—

$$v = \left\{ \frac{\cdot 8 \, d^2 \, f \, s \, n}{w \cdot b \cdot d} \right\} ; \text{ in which}$$

v expresses the required speed in knots per hour,

d = diameter of the steam-cylinder,

f = pressure in pounds by the Indicator,

s = length of stroke in feet,

n = number of cylinders,

w = diameter of the wheel in feet, minus $\frac{2}{3}$ of the immersed parts of lowest float-board,

b = breadth of the ship in feet,

d = draught of ditto, minus $\frac{1}{10}$th of b,

8 = a constant quantity.

attached to a spring balance; this rod is also attached
at the same end to another rod which is parallel to it,
and carries a pencil. A cylindrical barrel, whose axis
is parallel to this rod, is made to revolve, with the
screw-propeller, by means of straps going over pulleys,
so that the revolution of the barrel may be made
quicker or slower at pleasure; on the convex surface
of this barrel the pencil traces a line, straight or curved,
as described in the account of the indicator.

47. The spring balance is provided with an index and
a graduated scale; and the point at which the index
stands when the dynamometer is disconnected from the
screw-shaft is the zero of the scale, and a circle described
about the barrel in a plane perpendicular to its axis,
and through this point, is called the zero line. The
instrument being connected with the screw-shaft, the
revolutions of the barrel cause the pencil to describe an
undulating curve on one side of the zero line; and the
ordinates of the curve, being measured on a scale of
pounds formed on the strength of the spring balance,
give the number of pounds which denote the pressure
of the lever on the spring of the balance; a mean of
all these is to be taken, and this being multiplied by
the number expressing the ratio of the whole length of
the lever to the distance of the fulcrum from the end of
the screw-shaft, the product will be the pressure in
pounds exerted by the screw-shaft on the dynamometer,
and consequently, in the same (horizontal) direction,
on the vessel. The pressure, in pounds, thus exerted,
being multiplied by the velocity of the ship in feet per
minute, the product will be the number of dynamical
units in the effective power of the engine; and this,
divided by 33,000, will express the horse power.

The difference, if any, between this last and the
horse power obtained by the indicator, expresses (in
horse power) the loss of power in consequence of
friction, resistance, &c.

From the results of trials with these instruments it
has been found that the speed of a steam vessel varies
directly with the square root of the pressure on the

piston and with the cube root of the horse power of the engine. The *useful effect* of the engine, meaning that which remains after deducting the power spent in overcoming friction, &c., is supposed to bear a constant ratio to the power developed in the cylinder commonly called the *indicated horse power*. It is further estimated that the speed of a vessel varies directly with the cube root of the horse power, and inversely with the area of the mid-ship section ; or, directly with the cube root of the horse power, and inversely with the cube root of the square of the vessel's displacement.

48. The term horse-power, where used to designate the registered horse-power, gives but a remote idea of what the capabilities of the engine really are, and differs from the term horse-power as originally used, which showed the actual power exerted by the engine ; it now merely serves to estimate approximatively the money to be paid for the engine, and by no means shows the actual amount of *working* horse-power. Mr. Atherton, in his work ' Steam-ship Capabilities,' shows this to be the case, and proves from a comparison of the nominal horse-power with the power actually produced in ten packets, that *a marine horse-power* may be represented by a pressure on the piston equivalent to 132,000 lbs. moving at the rate of one foot per minute. He therefore proposes to make that the unit of power expressed by the word *horse-power* in all cases, whether nominal or effective, as shown by a dynamometer.

49. Captain Ryder also, in his valuable work ' On the Economy of Fuel in Steam Engines,' shows that the known results of working steam expansively at a higher pressure than 7 lbs. on each square inch, the mechanism of the engine being at the same time in the best state of efficiency, should deter engineers from using the vague term *nominal horse-power*. The value of that power was, at the time of its introduction, obtained from the mean effective pressure in the engines of that day ; but it is far inferior to the value deduced from the greater and more efficient engines at present in use.

50. The circumstances which immediately led to the
introduction of the screw in the steam-vessels of the
Royal Navy were the competitive trials made in 1840
between the 'Archimedes' screw-ship, which had been
built in 1838, and the wheel-steamer 'Widgeon.' In
the first of these trials, four runs of 19 miles, from Dover
to Calais, and as many in return, during calm weather,
the 'Widgeon' accomplished the distance on an
average, in 5' 50" less time than the 'Archimedes;'
but in a run to Calais and the return, with a fresh
breeze and all sails set, the 'Archimedes' accomplished the distance on an average, in 7' 30" less time
than the 'Widgeon.' These trials were, however,
far from being decisive, and the ships were not well
matched, as the steam-power of the 'Archimedes' was
less than that of the 'Widgeon,' and her burthen
greater. In order, therefore, to test the relative values
of the screw and paddle, the 'Rattler' screw-ship was
put in competition with the 'Alecto' paddle-ship, both
of which had been built on the same lines, and, in the
relation of tonnage to horse-power, were considered as
nearly equal to one another.

51. The trials were made in the North Sea, in the year
1845. In five of them the two vessels were impelled
by steam only, and it was found that, whether moving
in a calm or on a wind, the advantage in speed was on
the side of the screw-ship in every trial except one.
The distances run varied from 34 to 80 miles, and the
mean excess of the 'Rattler's' speed over that of the
'Alecto' was half a knot per hour. In the excep-
tional case the 'Alecto' gained half a mile on the
'Rattler' in a run of about 30 miles. In three other
trials the two vessels were under sail only, the 'Alecto'
unshipping her paddles, and the 'Rattler' fixing the
blades of her screw right up and down; and, in all of
these, the speed of the 'Rattler' exceeded that of the
'Alecto,' as she accomplished a run greater in extent
by four miles in less time than the other ship by
40' 20", a circumstance which militates against the
supposition that the two ships were equal in qualities

independent of steam-power. In two trials the ships, under steam-power only, were made to tow each other, alternately, by the head; and, on comparing the results, it was found that the mean speed of the 'Rattler' exceeded that of the 'Alecto' by 1½ knots per hour. Lastly, in one trial, the two ships were connected together stern to stern, and the engines of both were put in action with their maximum power; the result was still in favour of the screw-propeller.

52. In commenting on these experimental trips it is proper to remark that in heavy weather, and with a head-sea, a great deal of power was occasionally lost to the 'Rattler' by the screw being thrown quite out of the water. Again, the same vessel had, occasionally, a difficulty in obtaining steam, a circumstance which may have been caused by want of air in the engine-room, from some defect in its construction. The engines of the 'Rattler' were new, while those of the 'Alecto' had been five years in use. These trials are stated to have afforded some evidence of a greater amount of helm-power in the screw-ship over the paddle-steamer; and this is what might be expected, since the screw is placed at the stern of the vessel, and its movement must cause a powerful stream of water to be forced against the rudder.

53. Some interesting trials were subsequently made between the 'Rattler' screw-ship, and the 'Prometheus' paddle-steamer, in which the engines of both ships had the same horse power, and the ships were laden to equal draughts of water, 11 feet 3 inches. The distance run was a measured mile in Long Reach; and in these the advantage was in favour of the screw-ship, whose speed was 10¾ miles per hour, while that of the paddle-ship was only 10⅕ miles per hour.

54. In two trials made in the Channel, in 1849, between the 'Basilisk' paddle-ship and the 'Niger' screw-steamer (on board of which at the time was the author's son, now Capt. Douglas, R.N.), both vessels under steam and sail, the wind being *a-beam* during one trial, and *aft* during the other, the 'Basilisk' gained over

the 'Niger,' in the first case, 1796 fathoms, and in the second 3360 fathoms. The next day, both ships being under sail only, and on a wind, the 'Niger' gained over the 'Basilisk' in one trial 5756·6 fathoms, and in the other 5258 fathoms.

55. On another occasion the two ships were set to tow one another a-head, when, in two trials, the 'Basilisk' (paddle) had the advantage; the rates of towing and the consumption of fuel being as follow :—

Rates of Towing.	Consumption of Fuel per Day.
Basilisk . 7·65 and 6·0 knots.	Basilisk . 39·6 and 36·9 tons.
Niger . . 4·8 and 5·63 ,,	Niger . . 52·2 and 53·6 ,,

56. The ships were subsequently made to act against one another stern to stern; and in this operation the power of the 'Niger' (screw) was found to be the greatest : this vessel drew the 'Basilisk' at the rate of 1·466 knots per hour, while the 'Basilisk' drew her at the rate of 1 knot only per hour.

In these trials the 'Niger' laboured under many disadvantages ; her furnaces and boilers were defective, and the valves were frequently out of order. Her consumption of fuel was so great that she could not steam so far as the 'Basilisk' in the same time.[a] It is stated that, whenever the 'Niger' could get the steam, she always beat the 'Basilisk.'

57. The following remarkable experiment, which seems at first sight to disprove the supposition that the power of the screw is diminished by the eddy, and the cross actions of the water on the blades of a screw at the stern of a ship, was made by the 'Bee' steamer, which was furnished with wheel paddles and a screw, both of which were put in motion by the same engine at the same time. In the first trial the ship was impelled forward (the paddles being a-head and the screw a-stern), when the dynamometer registered 373 lbs. in favour of the paddles. Afterwards, the vessel was impelled

---

[a] Her consumption of fuel was about 52 tons, while that of the 'Basilisk' was only about 24 tons, in 24 hours.

in the contrary direction, the screw ahead and the paddles astern; the result was the same as before in favour of the paddles.   Little dependence can, however, be placed on this experiment; and the cause of the agreement in the results of the trials is ascribed to the circumstance that the paddles required a smaller speed, and the screw one much higher, to develope their best effects; consequently the screw was always going much slower than it ought to go in order to do its work, and therefore did not do it faithfully.   It should be added that the 'Bee' is too shallow a vessel for the purpose, experience having shown that ships deep in the water are more effectually acted upon by the screw than those of less draught.

58. Though in almost every experiment the *screw* appears to have advantages over the *wheel* in respect of the speed with which it moves a ship, the advantages, even in this respect, were not sufficiently decisive to obviate a doubt whether they might not have been due to accidental circumstances, particularly to the want of equality in the powers of the engines employed, and in the moving qualities of the ships themselves.[a]   To eliminate these causes of uncertainty it would be necessary not only to repeat the trials, but to use greater precautions in selecting for the trials, ships which might be more equally matched.   Even were the superiority of screw-steamers more clearly proved, it would not be proper to supersede the wheel-steamers entirely.   The disadvantages of these last, with respect to gunnery power, do not exist in vessels intended for mercantile and packet service; and for these services large and powerful wheel-steamers have been constructed, which, properly armed, would form most important vessels for the purposes of war.   In making future trials, the points particularly to be attended to should be the comparative capabilities of the wheel and screw to contend with heavy gales, their relative values with

---

[a] 'Niger' and 'Basilisk' were as far as possible sister ships, with the same nominal horse power.

respect to steerage power in the ships, and as auxiliaries
to the sail.

59. It is certain that a screw, except when the ship is
small and has much pitching motion, is never exposed
above water to an enemy's shot, but it may be doubted
whether, from the propinquity of the screw to the stern-
post and rudder, the damage the ship might receive
would not be more injurious than that which would be
produced by a shot striking a wheel ; the whole stern of
a screw-steamer forms a broad target exposed to fire,
which, supposing good gunnery on the part of the enemy,
might, by the stern-post being disabled or carried away,
cause the screw to be put out of service, and perhaps
the shaft broken by the overhanging weight of the
steerage apparatus. In small screw-steamers, the propelling shaft may be made to bear on a collar in the
main stern-post, instead of passing through it, and
by this construction any damage done to the outer
sternpost would not much affect the action of the
machinery ; but with the larger screws, weighing from
four to eight or ten tons, a bearing on the outer
stern-post becomes indispensable. It is remarkable
that, as far as present experience goes, the paddle-
wheel escapes, in a wonderful manner, the action of
shot ; and it remains to be proved whether or not the
sterns of screw ships, in which the rudder, rudder-
case, trunk, yokes for steering, the inner and outer
sternpost, all lie in close propinquity, will be equally
fortunate.

60. In order to avoid the necessity of a screw-steamer
going into dock whenever an accident happens to the
screw itself, all the screw-ships in Her Majesty's service
are now provided with *trunks* or quadrangular apertures, through which a screw may be hoisted up and
repaired, or even replaced by a spare screw. The
trunk at T, fig. 6, p. 68, being in a situation which
prevents the employment of an ordinary tiller, it
becomes necessary to provide a particular apparatus for
steering the ship ; this consists of a yoke A C B, fig. 6,
fixed to the stem D of the rudder, to which the requisite

motions are given by means of tackles from the ends A and B of the yoke, passing through pulleys inserted in a beam astern of it, leading on each side of the trunk or propeller-well T, to the steering-wheel on the quarter-deck.

Fig. 6 a represents an elevation of the upper part of a rudder, and shows the positions of two yokes, E F and I K, one on each deck; one of these is called a *preventive tiller*, and is intended to be used in the event of the other being destroyed.

61. Messrs. Maudslay and Field have lately made for H. M. S. 'Marlborough' a screw with blades of the ordinary form, bolted by flanges into the central axis, the bolt holes through the flanges being elongated, so as to admit of the obliquity of the blades to a vertical plane being altered. When the bolts are slackened, the blades may be turned round as far as may be required, and the bolts may then be tightened in order to fix the blades fast in their altered position. A comparatively slight alteration of the angle is sufficient to make a considerable difference in the speed of the vessel, and the blades may be set to that obliquity which is found under all circumstances to give the greatest speed to the ship. The peculiar advantages of this description of propeller are as follow:

1st.—To enable a vessel fitted with it to proceed under canvas alone, without the necessity of the screw being raised out of the water, and without the immersion of the screw offering any resistance to the onward progress of the ship.

This is accomplished by placing the faces of the blades fore and aft, in a vertical plane passing through the keel.

2nd.—An alteration of the angle of the blades at pleasure, to suit the varied circumstances under which the screw may be employed, which is of especial advantage in long voyages, when sailing and steaming are combined; it also admits of a great saving in the consumption of fuel, and a high speed of vessel being maintained.

By altering the angle of the blades the screw may
be made to advance through the water with greater
facility, and with a reduced number of revolutions
on its axis : thus following up the speed obtained by
the ship under canvas, and using the engines as an auxiliary power only.

The alterations in the position of the blades may be
effected in a few minutes, from the deck, by mechanical
means, while the vessel is under way, by one man, and
in any weather.

Whatever the comparative advantages or disadvantages of the paddle and the screw, applied to the propulsion of ships of war, may be, the screw possesses so
many advantages over the paddle as to give it a decided
preference for general purposes.

62. The screw admits of a better, stronger, and
more simple form of vessel. Relieved of the paddle-
boxes, the screw-propelled vessel is far less acted
upon by head-winds, and less subject to the heavy
rolling motion occasioned and aggravated by the
oscillations consequent on the top-weights on both
sides of a paddle-wheel vessel when the boxes receive
the impulses and surges of the sea — such oscillations being highly unfavourable to gunnery. The
screw is little affected by alterations in the trim
of the ship, it is very nearly equally effective at all
depths of immersion, and if entirely submerged, it
may be driven by the direct action of engines placed
so low in the vessel that both the moving power and
the propelling machinery are safe from the damaging
effects of shot : the screw allows more freely the use of
sails, and consequently enables the vessel to which it is
applied to retain her faculties as a sailing-ship in a
much higher degree than paddle-wheels ; it admits of
considerable reduction in the beam or breadth of the
vessel, which, besides other advantages, is an important
consideration in the economy of space, in a basin or in
dock, and with respect to the magnitude of the flood-
gates through which it has to pass. To which advantages may be added, that the decks of screw-propelled

vessels are wholly available for broadside armament, and admit of full gunnery power being retained.

63. But the screw-propeller, to be effective, requires that the shaft be driven with great rotatory speed to enable it to put forth its maximum power. To effect this, "*gearing*" or bands, and the drum, have heretofore been much resorted to in order to multiply the revolutions of the propelling shaft, but both have been found inconvenient. The slip of the band in the experiments with the 'Rattler' amounted to no less than 2·7 per cent.; and the inconvenience of gearing consists in the impossibility of placing the machinery below the water-line.[a]

For these and other reasons, engines acting directly on the cranks of the propelling shaft have been introduced, and will, no doubt, be generally employed.

In Penn's engine, oscillating cylinders have direct actions on the piston-rods, by which means the cross strains produced by fixed cylinders on the rods are obviated.

64. But direct action is not without its disadvantages. In consequence of the increased velocity given to the pistons, the diameter of the cylinder is made less than the usual standard, and the steam and eduction passages are unusually large in a condensing engine. The limit to the velocity at which the pistons may be worked is determined by the velocity of the water drawn out by the air-pump; and it appears that a velocity of 110 to 120 feet per minute—the maximum allowed according to Boulton and Watt's standard—is the greatest that can be given to the pump with safety. When the velocity of the water exceeds this, the air-pump-bucket communicates to the water a series of blows, the shock of which is very destructive to the material, the valve strikes hard, and the end of the screw-shaft is thrown upon its collars with great strain to it and to the piston rods. Various appliances have been tried to diminish the violence of the shocks to which the water is subjected, but, with fixed cylinders, nothing to remedy

---

[a] The engine now drives the screw without either drum or gearing.

the strains on the piston-rods acting directly on the cranks of the propelling shafts has been discovered; and, for this reason, oscillating cylinders, such as were used many years ago for paddle-wheel vessels, are now generally applied, for the direct action, in large steamers of war.

Another disadvantage in the screw, which it has not been found possible to remove, is the heat caused by friction when the number of revolutions made by the shaft per minute amounts to 60 or 70; the weight of the screw being from three to four tons, and in large ships six to eight tons, that friction becomes very great.

65. Among the anomalies in steam navigation which practice has exhibited, may be mentioned the fact that screw-vessels, though full in the quarter, steer remarkably well, contrary to what is observed with sailing vessels and with wheel-steamers—a circumstance which is caused by the current of water from the screw acting on the rudder with considerable force. To the same cause must be ascribed the fact that screw-vessels, even with full after-bodies, have, in general, less *slip* than other vessels. In the experimental trials made by H. M. S. ' Plumper,' the slip was found to be negative; that is, the water aft of the screw, instead of receding from it, moved towards it, thus increasing the screw's power of giving motion to the vessel. In eleven trials made by that ship, in running a measured mile in Stokes Bay, the speed of the vessel always exceeded that which should be given by the power of the engine by 0·7 knots per hour on an average, the screw making from 83 to 115 revolutions per minute. In going *head to wind*, the slip of the screw has been thought to increase in a higher ratio than that of the paddle-wheel, but the experiments have not, as yet, been sufficiently numerous and precise to determine this point.

66. A screw-vessel clean in the *run* is apparently the most advantageous. The ' Dauntless,' steam-frigate, when tried in August, 1848, in running a measured mile, had a speed of 7·36 miles per hour. Subsequently an additional length of eight feet at the stern was

given her, in order to carry the rudder farther out of the eddy; the speed was found to be 10·266 miles per hour; the vessel being under steam only in all the trials.

67. The relative consumption of fuel in steamers of different kinds is a subject of very great importance, and, in any one steamer, it is found to vary with the vessel's draught of water and with the cube of its velocity; consequently, when a high speed is obtained, the consumption will be very great, a double velocity being produced, *cæteris paribus*, by an eight-fold quantity of fuel. Hence it follows that when the necessity of the service does not imperatively require great speed, a due economy would be obtained by keeping the vessel as much as possible at a low rate of motion. The minimum speed of steamers is seldom less than 3 miles per hour; a less velocity would require the power of the engine to be so far diminished that it would scarcely turn the shaft.

68. It is now proved that, in steam navigation, a greater amount of locomotive power is obtained by means of the paddle-wheels than by means of the screw, with an equal consumption of fuel; of the two kinds of vessels, when moved by steam only, one with paddle-wheels can, therefore, keep the sea a longer time, or perform service of longer duration, than one of the other kind; but the advantages are on the side of the screw when steam is used in both, in conjunction with, or as an auxiliary to the sail.

69. If two steamers equal in every respect, except that one is equipped with paddle-wheels and the other with a screw, are moving under sail only, with equal velocities, any required increase of speed will be obtained from steam with less expenditure of fuel by a screw, than by a paddle-wheel ship; and the fact may be accounted for by considering that the water on which a screw acts being under the stern is almost in a state of rest relatively to the ship, whereas, along the sides, where the wheels act, it is virtually receding at a rate equal to the ship's movement; and consequently a greater number of revolutions of the wheels than of the

screw, in a given time, must be made in order to obtain
an equal increase of speed for the vessels.

70. Economy of fuel may be gained by working steam
very expansively. But the expansive process cannot
long be continued ; inasmuch as the expansion is attended with diminished pressure, which causes a diminution of speed ; and therefore, the economy does not
exist when a given distance is to be run in a limited
time.

71. In experiments made by the ' Bee,' which was
fitted up to work either with screw or wheel, 42 revolutions of the screw only produced a velocity equal
to 6·8 miles per hour, while 32 revolutions of the
wheel-shaft produced a speed of 7·5 miles per hour ;
the consumption of steam, and consequently of fuel,
being proportional to the number of revolutions of the
shafts. Likewise, in the trials between the ' Rattler '
and the ' Alecto,' where the advantage of speed was in
favour of the former ship, the revolutions of the screw
were, to those of the paddle-wheels, in the ratio of 24 to
19 very nearly, and the consumptions of fuel were, of
course, in the same proportion.

72. It is evident that, when the object is to attain a
given distance, steam may be worked expansively,
with different degrees of expansion according to circumstances : with a given increase of time an economy
of fuel may be obtained by a greater space for expansion ; and conversely a given diminution of time may
be obtained by less space for expansion, which would
require an increased consumption of fuel.

73. The *shake* of the screw and the consequent injury
to the stern of the ship, as mentioned in Art. 38, are
caused by the sudden and violent reactions of the disturbed water in that place against the blades of the
screw as they enter and emerge from thence.[a] The

---

[a] In consequence of the metal covering of the screw-shaft breaking loose on
board the ' Royal Albert,' during her passage from the Black Sea to Malta, in
1855, by which the *tubing* in the stern-post was torn away, and the *gland* and
stuffing-box were forced off, so great a quantity of water rushed into the ship
that it was necessary to lay her aground in order to prevent her from sinking

rectilinear edges A B and G H, fig. 4, of the ordinary screws, are, in this respect, highly disadvantageous, since the whole of an edge enters and leaves at once the water on each side of the aperture ; within which aperture the water is (Art. 32, p. 37) comparatively in a quiescent state ; but if the leading edges of a screw-blade were curved, as A′p B, G p′H′, they would slide obliquely and continuously through the water, like a screw formed with an entire feather, so that, at no moment, would there be any shock or discontinuity of action. The curved edges have, besides, the advantage of readily throwing off any

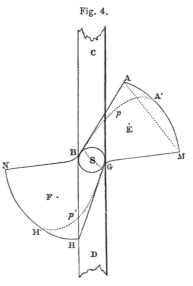

Fig. 4.

floating materials that may come in contact with them, and are not so liable to be broken by their oblique collision with large spars, as straight edges are by their direct blow ; while the angular parts of the common screw are far more likely to be hitched by ropes than the rounded extremities of the other. If these curved parts could be furnished with sharp knife-edges, partly notched like saws, and made of a metal capable of resisting the corroding effects of sea-water, or could be frequently removed and cleaned, they would be capable of

---

in deep water. A similar accident occurred to the Peninsular mail-steamer 'Alhambra,' in her last voyage ; the stuffing which closes the orifice at the stern of the ship, through which the shaft is connected with the screw, got away, and let in so much water as to render it necessary to keep the pumps going during the remainder of the voyage. Besides the severe and well nigh fatal catastrophe which happened to the 'Royal Albert,' the 'Crecy,' 'Colossus,' and many other screw steam-ships of the line had become so leaky in the after part of their *clear runs*, through the caulking being loosened by the constant tremor and vibration occasioned by the screw, as to require to be taken into dock.

dividing any rope, spar, or other floating matter, like a powerful circular saw. C D represents the sternpost of a screw-steamer, B G the boss of the screw; and the direction in which the screw revolves is according to the order of the letters M A N H.[a]

It will be easily understood that until such a form shall be given to the screw as that it may exert a continuity of action, it will be in vain to expect that shocks should cease to take place. The author would not, at the sacrifice of speed, revert to a continuous feather-screw; but the form here recommended would, to a considerable extent, gain the proposed ends: if, also, the edges of the blades were chamfered, the shock produced as they pass through the water would be further diminished.

The curved lines in the above figure being traced within the straight lines A B, G H, which represent the edges of a common screw: it follows that a screw so formed will be of a somewhat diminished breadth; but it is understood that a small diminution of breadth causes no sensible diminution of the propelling power of the screw. A loss of power might be obviated by tracing the curves so as to give the blades a greater breadth than that of the common screw; but this is not to be recommended; and it will be found advantageous to have the blades of a screw as narrow as possible, consistent with an adequate propelling power. The screw of a large ship weighs from 8 to 10 or 12 tons; and when a ship pitches much in a heavy sea, the screw is sometimes quite out of the water; in this case, the resistance being taken off, the screw revolves with such

---

[a] The dotted line A p p' H' will show that, with blades so formed, there is a continuity of action on the water, though the screw itself be divided into two parts.

The screw lately invented by Mr. Griffiths, the blades of which diminish both in the fore and aft, and in the transverse direction, has some advantages over that which is in common use; it allows the aperture in which it works, and the trunk, to be of smaller dimensions, thus rendering the parts about the stern of the ship stronger; but it may be doubted whether the narrowness of the blades may not be the cause of a sensible diminution of the propelling power.

rapidity as to endanger the stability of the whole machinery, as often happens in merchant steamers forcing their way in long voyages against adverse winds and heavy seas. To provide against this evil—and the subject concerns as much the mercantile as the warlike navy of the country—the blades of the screw, and consequently the aperture in which it works, as well as the trunk through which it is occasionally drawn up, should be as much as possible reduced, and also the parts of the ship about the stern should be much strengthened, to enable them to resist the great strains to which they are liable. That this should be done effectually is plainly an affair of the highest national importance.

74. The screw is, in general, less exposed than a wheel to injury from objects floating in the water; yet in a crowded anchorage it is liable to become entangled with warps, nets, and the like; and any expedient by which the screw might be guarded from being so entangled and disabled, would obviously be of vast importance to the efficiency of a steam-ship.

75. The instances of screws getting foul by ropes, nets, &c., wound up tightly on their bosses are too numerous to admit of notice in detail. The screw of the 'Exmouth,' ship of the line was fouled by her own sheet cable, in endeavouring to haul herself off a shoal, for which she had laid out an anchor; the cable was wound up so tightly that there was very great difficulty and much delay in clearing the screw.

The screw steam-ship 'Melbourne,' formerly the 'Greenock,' on her voyage to Australia in 1852, was taken in a gale of wind, by which she was partially dismasted; her screw was fouled and disabled by the wreck of her own rigging; and being thus deprived of both powers of motion, sails and screw, she lay like a log on the sea, and put into Plymouth for repair.

When the 'Tribune' was docked at Sheerness on the 10th June, 1853, it was found that 11 fathoms of 3½-inch rope had been wound up on the boss of her

screw in such a manner as must have disabled the
machine if the rope had been much longer. Before the
' Rattler ' set out on her trial trip with the ' Alecto,'
Art. 51, it was found that a 7-inch hawser had been
closely wound, together with some fishing-nets, about
her screw, and it was several hours before a complete
clearance could be effected. And numerous cases occur
in which the screw-propellers of ships were discovered,
when the ships were docked, to have wound up on
their screws, ropes, fragments of nets or sails, lead
and log lines.

76. The entanglements of screws in the open sea
occur rarely compared with the foulings which take
place in rivers, harbours, and roadsteads; but when
steam-ships, in *line ahead*, are in action, the risk of, and
the detriment arising from, their screws getting fouled
by the rigging shot away, are very great; the wreck
getting into the wake of the ships, or, passing these,
floating into the course of those astern of them. On
this account, any means by which the unimpaired
action of screw-propellers may be insured is a matter
of very high importance.

77. If there were no probability of a screw-propeller
being disabled in action, and consequently no necessity
for being prepared to resort to the sail, a great deal of
the running rigging might be removed, the topgallant
and royal yards, all the topgallant studdingsail and
royal gearing sent down from the tops, and even the
topgallant masts might be struck, in order to lessen the
chance of rigging shot away, falling from aloft, and
getting adrift in the sea ; thereby fouling the screw, and
rendering the vessel with all her armament immovable
except by the sail.

78. After bestowing the most serious consideration on
the subject of a fouled screw, and on the various expedients
by which it has been attempted to remedy this great evil,
the author has arrived at the conclusion, that the clearing
of a screw can only be effected by some contrivance that
may enable screw-propellers to clear themselves of any

ropes or other floating wrecks of rigging which may hitch upon a blade in its rotation, and which being drawn down to the root of the blade would be wound up on the boss so tightly as ultimately to disable the propeller, or derange the driving machinery, if the engine were not immediately stopped. For clearing the screw the author proposes to employ strong and sharp steel knife-edges firmly fixed to the metal trunk in which the screw works, and close to both edges of the blade, in such a manner that any rope that may have hitched on the boss would be acted upon, during the revolution of the screw, as a body revolving in a turning-lathe is acted upon by a chisel. Thus revolving with a force derived from the power of the engine, the rope must be drawn into and along the knife-edges, causing these to exert a drawing cut, sufficient to sever any rope, whatever be its thickness, and so clear the screw at once of any such entanglement as those shown in the annexed (fig. 5).

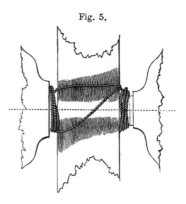

Fig. 5.

Should the force with which the rope so hitched is drawn under the knife-edges appear to create an injurious strain on the square end of the propelling shaft, the object may be accomplished by means of circular fixed cutters acting in a direction parallel to the shaft; the cylindrical parts of the boss, between the blades of the screw, being brought under the cutters as the screw revolves. The corrosive effects of salt-water on the cutters might be obviated by cleaning the edges, the screw being, for this purpose, temporarily removed.

Before he quits this subject, the author would suggest that a screw-propeller might be examined at any time, either at anchor or under way in a smooth sea, by sending an experienced diver in the diving-dress down the well on a step-ladder, to the boss; the blades

of the screw being laid horizontally, the man, furnished
with a knife, might cut the bight which had hitched
round a blade, on the boss; and taking with him from
the deck a line, he might fasten it to either of the loose
ends of the rope that had been wound up; then ascending to the deck, the screw being turned in the reverse
direction, the rope that had been wound up would be
wound off: for this an experienced diver, air-pump,
and diving-dress should be provided in every screw-
ship.   In this manner the evil of a fouled screw may be
removed.

The importance of having on board of at least one
of the ships in a fleet of screw-steamers, a diver, with
the necessary apparatus, for the purpose of descending
to the axle of a screw, in the event of any accident
occurring to that part of the machinery, is evident from
a circumstance which took place in July, 1854, when a
fleet of British men-of-war was lying in Calais Roads,
having on board 10,000 French troops, who afterwards
assisted at the taking of Bomarsund.   Shortly before
the time appointed for raising the anchors, it was found
that the screw of the flag-ship, the 'Hannibal,' had
become deranged, and would not work.   On this
occasion a helmet-diver from the works at Dover was
sent across the Straits : this man, by means of a rope-
ladder, went down the *trunk*, and in about three hours
succeeded in re-establishing the screw; and the troops
were thus enabled to start at the time appointed.   The
accident arose from the screw getting foul in the
vertical guides, so that it would neither lift nor lower ;
and was caused from the vessel touching the sill when
she left the dock in which she was repaired, and which
wrung or twisted the metal guides in which the screw
worked.   If the injury had not been thus repaired,
the 'Hannibal' must have returned to port, and gone
into dock.

The screw of the 'Blenheim' also, while that ship
was in the Baltic, became fouled by one of the hawsers,
and entirely disabled ; and on this occasion a trained

diver, sent down from the deck, produced an effectual clearance.[a]

79. The author's object in what he has stated has been chiefly to engage the mechanical genius of English artists to apply itself to the means of preventing the shake produced by the screw, and of enabling the latter to clear itself of the obstructions to which it is liable; and it would afford him the greatest possible satisfaction, to find that the methods by which he proposes to gain these ends are superseded by some more effectual expedient than he has been able to discover. British mechanical skill has taken the lead, which it should ever retain, in working out the problem of the application of steam to the propulsion of ships of war, and carried the machinery to the highest degree of perfection which, in the present state of science and art, the case admits of; but it must not be concluded that the problem is so satisfactorily solved as not to admit of further improvement, though it is not at present easy to show how this is to be effected.

The sterns of all ships are still their weakest parts, notwithstanding the great improvements made in naval construction of late years, by abolishing the wing transoms upon which the stern-frame was built, and substituting, as in the construction of the bows, timbers rising from the keel, thus uniting the whole body of the ship in an entire frame; yet the overhanging stern not being water-borne, in consequence of the fine run below, this part of every ship is rendered weaker than the bows; and the aperture made in the dead wood, together with the openings called the well, extending from the head of that aperture through all the decks above, weakens farther the part already much deficient in strength. Hence the violent shocks occasioned

---

[a] The author has recently learned that, on board the 'Excellent,' seamen are now regularly trained to act as divers; these, when duly qualified, receive additional pay, and are provided with the necessary dress and apparatus. This circumstance, for which great credit is due to the naval administration of the country, was unknown to the author till after the present sheet was in type.

by the rotations of a heavy screw-propeller, occurring
in quick succession, strain the stern to a degree which,
in a short time, endangers the stability of the whole
fabric. The steerage of the ship is greatly impeded
by the intervention of the trunk, which renders it impossible to use a long tiller, and permits only the sub-
stitution of two short arms of a lever, called a yoke,
which works within the small space between the trunk
and the stern.

Figures 6 and 6 a represent the steering-apparatus of
a screw steam-ship of 91 guns. G, fig. 6 a, is the head

Fig. 6.

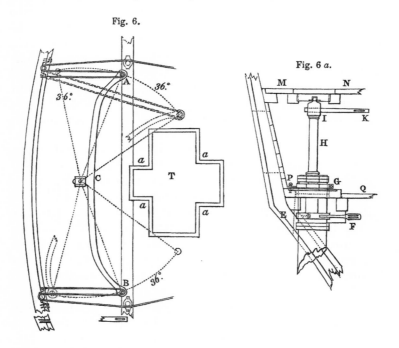

Fig. 6 a.

of the rudder, of which the upper and smaller part H,
called the Norman head, is a strong iron column (with
a hole for the reception of the tiller or yoke, I K, at
the upper part) which ships into a square mortice in
the rudder-head at G, strengthened by strong iron
bands, as shown in fig. 6 a. The rudder is acted upon

by means of a yoke, A B C fig. 6 (I K, fig. 6 a), on the main deck, and by a similar yoke E F, on the lower deck, by either of which the ship may be steered. Each yoke consists of two arms, straight or curved, which are worked by tackles made fast to, and rove through a stern-beam, and can be moved through an angle of 36 degrees in either direction. When additional power on the helm is required, it is obtained by means of relieving-tackles, consisting of double blocks, one of which is attached to each arm of the yoke, and the other to the side of the ship. The lower yoke E F works underneath and close to the beams of the main deck P Q (fig. 6 a), and the upper yoke I K close under the beams of the quarter-deck M N.[a]

The arms of the yoke being short, compared with the length of an ordinary tiller, it has been found necessary, in order to obtain sufficient power to turn the rudder, to have a multiplying purchase, consisting of a system of pulleys near the end of each arm of the yoke, and also in a main beam in its rear; the rope, or rather the chain (for a rope, though made of prepared hide, is soon worn through), is made fast to the yoke, and passes round a sheave in the beam behind; then round one in the arm of the yoke; and, after passing about a second sheave in the beam, it is carried to the barrel of the steering-wheel on the quarter-deck. In consequence of the complexity of this apparatus, a considerable revolving motion of the steering-wheel is necessary in order to produce even a small movement of the rudder; and there is, therefore, a want of promptitude in the corrective power of the helm, when moved by the yoke, which is not experienced when a ship is steered by a simple tiller in the ordinary way.

Various other modes of steering have been tried with the yoke and with a short tiller, as I K, fig. 6 a, fixed in front, or in the rear of the Norman head, but no satisfactory result has yet been obtained from them. Experiments are now being made at Portsmouth with

---

* In three-decked ships, the lower yoke is under the beams of the middle deck, and the upper yoke below the beams of the upper deck.

a tiller shipped to a cross-head on the stem of the
rudder, and leading towards the *quarters* of the ship;
and this is worked by tackles in either direction.   But
these complicated expedients to compensate, by the
multiplicity of gearing, for the defects occasioned by
the absence of the long tiller, do but increase the evils
complained of, and are evidences of the necessity of
reverting to the use of that simple agent.

The great force of torsion exerted on the stem of the
rudder by the yoke on the lower deck, by the short
tiller in the Norman head, and sometimes by both
acting together, wrings the stem to such a degree that
many rudders have been entirely destroyed by it, and
it has been found necessary to provide against this
evil by giving additional strength to the rudder-heads
in all screw line-of-battle ships recently constructed.

Besides this injury to the rudder arising from the
employment of the yoke, the great force which it is
necessary to apply to the wheel in order to give motion
to the rudder, particularly when the latter is acted
upon by sudden and violent impulses from the striking
of waves against it, is also the cause that the steering
of screw-steamers, having trunks, is far less steady than
that of ships whose helms are managed by the ordinary
tiller.

The author has no personal experience in the art of
steering a steam-ship by the yoke, but he is enabled to
judge accurately on the subject by information obtained
from flag-officers who have inspected, captains who have
commanded, and officers who have served on board
screw-steamers, as well as from experienced quarter-
masters who have performed the mechanical operation of steering such ships : all these admit that the
trunk, from the space it occupies—not less than 243
cubic feet on each deck—has rendered it necessary to
resort to that disadvantageous means of giving motion
to the rudder ; but, believing it to be unavoidable, they
accept it as a necessary evil.   But is it necessary?
Why should a structure so detrimental to the steering
power of the ship, and so obstructive to the general
service of the decks, be suffered permanently to remain,

since its use is only occasionally required ?   Apertures must be made in all the decks to admit of the screw being hoisted up for the purpose of repairing it, or of replacing it by another.   In the latter case, the spare propeller (screw) is brought out of the stowage-bed in the hold, and transported aft on a suitable sledge.   The tackle by which the screw is hoisted consists of a double system of pulleys suspended from a strong timber (chock) spanning the aperture in the upper deck : each *fall* is made fast at one end to an immoveable object ; passing then over a friction-pulley in the chock, it is led under a pulley fixed to the metal frame which carries the screw, and is passed from thence over another friction-pulley in the chock to the barrel of the capstan : by heaving on this the metal frame, with the screw, is raised through the trunk to the upper deck.   When the screw is damaged and requires to be replaced or repaired, shears are erected of sufficient altitude to hoist the screw entirely clear of the aperture ; the frame with the screw is then lowered to the deck, when what is amiss may be repaired, or the screw may be replaced by a spare one.   While this operation is being performed, which is accomplished in ten or twelve minutes after the gearing is prepared, the long tiller cannot, of course, be used ; this must, therefore, be unshipped and triced up to the beams, and the yoke or short tiller must be applied for the purpose of steering the ship till the screw is refixed ; but it must be unnecessary to enclose the apertures by permanent bulkheads.   Might it not suffice to carry the trunk up from the top of the aperture in which the screw works, as high as the lower-deck, and no higher ?   To prevent the surge of the sea, up the permanent trunk, from getting into the lower deck, a strong cap of timber should be made to close the aperture, the chain attached to the screw being passed through a hole perforated in the centre of the cover, and kept ready to be passed through the apertures in the decks above, when the operation of hoisting the screw is required.   When the screw is to be hoisted up, temporary stanchions might be fixed in mortices at the four corners of the rectangular

space (*a a* fig. 6) to which the boss must be confined in
moving the screw up and down ; and by these stanchions
the edges of the metal frame in which the screw is set
may, in lowering it, be conducted into the metal guides
fixed vertically in the permanent trunk below the lower
deck, so as to bring it, as before, to the proper place
for connecting the screw with the propelling shaft.
By suppressing the trunk, the decks would be free for
the movements of a tiller of the ordinary length and
description, which, like the yokes, might be placed
immediately under the beams of the quarter-deck and
main deck respectively : the apertures being covered
by shutters, on which guns might be placed, the stern
batteries on each deck would be strengthened by the
two guns which the trunk had rendered useless ; and
thus spaces of about 700 and 1000 cubic feet, in two
and three deck ships respectively, would be restored to
the gun and ward room accommodation, and to the
apartments appropriated to the captain and the admiral.

The great advantage of applying screw-propulsion
to ships of war consists in these being enabled to
execute, with the utmost precision and certainty, the
tactical movements which the new system of naval
warfare will introduce. But that precision in execution
depends entirely upon the accuracy with which the
new moving power is directed by the helm ; and so
indispensable is correct steering in the evolutions of
steam-fleets, that the full benefit which steam propulsion is capable of affording cannot be obtained without
it. The reader will see, in the sequel of this work, the
immense importance of steady and correct steering in
the evolutions of steam-fleets ; and naval officers, in
practising the new and delicate manœuvres of which
the author is about to treat, will find that the most
serious consequences will result from any defect in the
apparatus by which steam-ships are steered.

The steering of a screw steam-ship of the line, with
all sails furled, should be as if instinct with life, in-
tuitive, and quick as volition. The more simple and
direct the regulating power of the helm is, the more it
will conform with the above attributes.

SECTION II.

On the Tactics of Naval Warfare with Steam.

80. The tactics of naval warfare under the power of
steam cannot be advantageously studied except in comparison with those in which the movements of the ships
depend on the action of the wind ; and it, therefore,
will be necessary to begin by a short description of the
elementary principles which have governed the operations of hostile fleets in past times, when the manœuvring powers of the sail alone could be employed
to effect the requisite evolutions.   The nature of these
evolutions being explained, it is proposed to enter upon
a description of the means of executing them, and of
the modifications which must be made in the tactics of
naval warfare when ships are moved by the power of
steam.

81. The science of naval warfare may be classed
under two principal divisions :—the order of movement
in advance or retreat, and the order of battle.

In 1697 Paul Hoste [a] published his treatise of Naval
Evolutions ; and this work, which was reprinted in
1727, is, by all writers on the art, pronounced to be
the ground on which succeeding theories have been
based.[b]

82. With respect to the first of these divisions,

---

[a] Father Paul l'Hoste, a Jesuit, was born at Bresse in 1652, and died Professor of Mathematics in the Royal College of Marine, at Toulon, in 1700,
aged 48.   He was present in many of the battles he describes, having served
for many years with some of the most distinguished admirals of France.   He
was on board the Count de Tourville's ship at the battle of La Hogue in 1692,
and served in some of the sanguinary battles fought between the English
and Dutch fleets in the 17th century.

[b] The principal writers on naval tactics since the time of Paul Hoste are :—
M. Bourde de Villehuit, 1769 ; M. de Moroques and M. du Pavillon, 1780 ;
Clarke of Eldon, 1790 ; Viscomte de Grenier, 1788 ; Steel, 1794 ; Admiral
Sir Charles Ekins' *Naval Battles.*

F

Paul Hoste enumerates six orders of sailing, which are as follow :—

1. *The line ahead* on the starboard or the port tack ; which is also the general order of battle.
2. *The line ahead* perpendicular to the wind.
3. On two *lines of bearing*,[a] when it is not known on what tack it will be necessary to engage.
4. In parallel columns or divisions before the wind.
5. In parallel columns oblique to the wind.
6. The order of retreat on two *lines of bearing*, making with each other an angle of 135°.

83. He afterwards dwells on the derangements which may be occasioned by changes of the wind occurring during an action, and on the manœuvres by which those changes should be met :—

1. The manner of re-establishing the line of battle when the wind comes ahead.
2. The manner of re-establishing the first order of sailing when the wind comes aft.
3. The manner of re-establishing the second order of sailing when the wind changes.
4. The manner of re-establishing the third and the fourth orders when the wind changes 16 points, or less than 16 points.
5. The manner of re-establishing the fifth order when the wind changes 4, 6, 8, or 12 points, and when the wind comes ahead.
6. The manner of re-establishing the order of retreat when the wind changes 4, 6, 8, 12, or 16 points.

To which he adds the manner of changing the order of battle to the different orders of sailing.

---

[a] Two lines of bearing are those in which the ships (at 6 points from the wind) are in lines, making with each other an angle of 135 degrees (see fig. 9, p. 93). From this order of sailing the line of battle can be promptly formed on either tack ; for one portion of the fleet is already in line ahead, and the other may be speedily brought to the same disposition, in the continuation of that line towards the rear.

84. In the tactics of sailing ships, the line of battle is formed by ranging the ships in *line ahead*, at 6 points from the wind, either on the starboard or the port tack.[a]

It has always been assumed, in preparing for an attack, that the fleet of the enemy is in *line ahead* close-hauled, to leeward or to windward; and by taking measures accordingly, with superior nautical skill and practical seamanship, the officers of the British navy have established and maintained for the country its supremacy on the ocean.

85. The intervals between ships in line of battle are never less than one cable's length, or 240 yards, but they may be at the distance of one and a half or even two cables' length. The ships are close-hauled to the wind, because in that trim the sails are easily made to counteract each other, by backing, filling, or shivering them, and thus the ships are easily kept in their proper stations. This can, with difficulty, be accomplished by the process of *bracing-by*,[b] when ships are going free, or before the wind.

The line of battle is not formed in a direction perpendicular to the wind, because, when ships so ranged make a tack, there is greater danger of each getting foul of her follower, in falling off upon the new tack, than when the ships are hauled to the wind.

The close-hauled lines form the normal condition upon which line of battle and all orders of sailing in lines of bearing are formed. In this state the conversion from the line of bearing to the line of battle might be simply and promptly made, subject to the limitations imposed by the wind.

86. The attack from the windward upon an enemy's fleet to leeward, is made by running down directly in line abreast, or obliquely in line of bearing,

---

[a] These are called in naval tactics close-hauled lines ; but square-rigged ships so ranged are one point *off* the wind.

[b] The method called *bracing-by* consists in turning the yards more or less obliquely to the wind, in order to discharge (spill) the wind from the sails, or to catch it on them, as the occasion may require.

each ship keeping its antagonist always on the same point of the compass. The windward fleet may thus, at any time, form a line parallel to that of the enemy, and may engage him at any distance ; or it may pass through his line of battle at one or more points, as Admiral Duncan did in the action off Camperdown, and as Lord Howe attempted to do on the 1st of June, 1794 ; or again, the weather-fleet may bear down in divisions in line ahead, and, penetrating the enemy's line, engage him to leeward, as Lord Nelson did in the battle off Cape Trafalgar.

The great solicitude which British admirals, in particular, have ever shown to gain the weather-gage, arose mainly from the option it gave to the commander of the windward fleet, either to force the enemy to a close action, or to compel him to edge away, bear up, and ultimately retreat.

87. The advantage of obtaining the weather-gage is strikingly illustrated in the description of the naval engagements between the English and Dutch fleets off the Texel, in 1653 and 1665 (Lediard's 'Naval History'), and in the action between the French and Dutch off Stromboli in 1676 (Charnock, vol. ii., p. 10), and in many more modern battles.

Fig. 7.

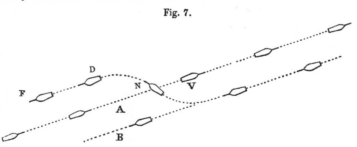

In the manœuvres of the British and French fleets on the 9th and 11th of April, 1782, Rodney's great object was to gain the weather-gage, but, being disappointed, he passed to leeward, engaging the enemy on the contrary tack ; when, taking advantage of a wide opening (A), fig. 7, made in the French line, through the ships astern of the 'Ville de Paris' having been so much damaged in their sails and rigging by the fire of the British van (B) as to be unable to keep their proper distances, he pushed the 'Formidable' (F), followed by the 'Duke' and 'Namur,' through the gap, doubled upon the French rear, and gained a complete victory.

Nelson's plan of attack for the action at Trafalgar was formed on the assumption that he should possess the advantage of being to windward, and thus have it in his power to penetrate the line of the combined French and Spanish fleets, by which manœuvre he contemplated engaging the enemy from the leeward, and preventing him from making his escape. (Clark's and MacArthur's 'Life of Nelson.')

88. In the leeward position of a fleet, the circumstances are very different from those which existed in the case above mentioned. A lee fleet cannot force into close action, one which is to windward of it; it might itself avoid such action by edging away, keeping up a distant cannonade on the enemy as he came down; but this manœuvre could produce no decisive result, and the affair might end in a drawn battle, of which we read many instances in naval history. It must be admitted, however, that in the case of inferior strength, the lee fleet has the advantage of its retreat being open, and may, accordingly, edge away, or retire before the wind.

A lee fleet cannot approach one to windward, each of them sailing close-hauled in line ahead upon the same tack; but if the lee fleet sails the fastest, it may *forereach* upon the other, and, then tacking, stand towards it. A windward fleet, close-hauled, can only be approached by a lee fleet fetching up, on the contrary tack, in line ahead; or, when having sufficiently forereached on the other, by making the ships tack simultaneously into line of bearing, parallel to the enemy, each ship stemming obliquely towards the enemy, and threatening to pass through the opposite interval. But in these cases the intervals in the enemy's line will be continually varying in their bearing and in their extent, by the relative celerities with which the ships are moving in contrary directions. Hence, in the attempt to break a line from the leeward, it must be uncertain which interval can be gained; and the extent of the interval is, practically speaking, diminished, from the obliquity of the line of penetration, while the leading ship or ships will be exposed to the broadside batteries of all the ships in the windward line, which are ahead of that part which it is intended to attack, as those ships pass in succession athwart the bows of the ships fetching up.

89. To penetrate an enemy's line from the leeward by the cross attack, as it is called (Art. 149), is impracticable, if the prescribed distances between the ships are accurately kept; and the manner of keeping the proper distance between two ships is here described for the information of the general reader. The mizen, or main-topsail (and topgallantsail, if set, or both occasionally), is kept shaking or backed, or more or less filled, if going upon a wind ; or *braced-by* if going large, so as either to check or increase the ship's speed. The interval from ship to ship, at the distance directed by signal, is regulated, by observing the angle subtended by the height of the mast-head above the water-line, of each nearest ship. The angles calculated for the different distances that may be signalled are entered in a table ; whence, by setting the index of a sextant to the angle corresponding to the distance ordered, it may be ascertained whether the ship is drawing ahead or dropping astern.

The issue of the battle of May 20, 1756, turned entirely upon an error in the order of sailing, by which the ' Intrepid,' with the loss of her foremast, drove on the ship next to that of the Admiral, and obliged the ships astern to throw all aback ; this caused so much delay that, night coming on, the French fleet bore off, and the action terminated, to the mortification of the country and the ruin of the admiral (Byng), in a drawn battle.

Instances in which attempts to break an enemy's line have ended in failure may be found in the accounts of the actions under Admiral Keppel in 1778, Lord

Howe in 1794,[a] Lord St. Vincent in 1797,[b] and Sir Robert Calder in 1805.

90. Steam propulsion entirely annuls all the limitations and disabilities imposed by the wind on the evolutions of fleets, and opens the whole surface of the ocean as a battle-field for the contests of steam fleets. With this new power it may be presumed that success will more than ever depend upon the tactical skill and the quick perception of the chief, together with prompt and resolute execution on the part of those under his command.

91. A fleet of steamers would experience, in breaking an enemy's fleet in line ahead, none of the difficulties to which sailing ships are subject from their dependence on the direction of the wind; but, with steam as a moving power, this manœuvre would not necessarily throw a fleet, commanded by a skilful tactician, into that inextricable disorder, nor reduce it to that state of utter helplessness, which in a sailing fleet has proved decisive of the fate of an action, as was the case on the 12th April, 1782. With a fleet whose facility of manœuvring quickly and precisely is great, as is that

---

[a] Lord Howe bore down with his whole fleet in line abreast, intending that every ship should pass through the enemy's line, and engage his ships to leeward, but the advance soon became disordered, and the Admiral was obliged to signal some ships to make more, and others less sail. The 'Queen Charlotte,' followed by the 'Bellerophon' and 'Leviathan,' passed unsupported through the French line astern of 'L'Eole,' and were with difficulty rescued from their perilous position; the remainder hauled their wind and opened fire, some at short, and others at long and scarcely effectual, distances. The 'Brunswick,' second ship to that of the Admiral, tried to cut through the line astern of the 'Jacobin,' the second to the French Admiral; but the 'Jacobin' ranged ahead, closely followed by the 'Achille,' so as not to leave sufficient space to pass through. The 'Brunswick,' thereupon, pushed for another opening between the 'Achille' and the 'Vengeur,' but the latter frustrated that design by shooting ahead and closing the interval. The 'Brunswick' persisting, ran foul of the 'Vengeur,' and the desperate battle which ensued between these two vessels, linked together by the 'Brunswick's' anchor getting hooked to the shrouds of the 'Vengeur'—a grasp which Captain Harvey would not release—forms a glorious episode in the history of the battle of the 1st June, 1794.

[b] In the battle of the 14th February, 1797, the three-decked ship 'Le Prince des Asturies,' leading the squadron of eight Spanish ships which had been separated from the principal division by the British fleet, endeavoured to pass through the British line, ahead of the 'Victory,' to reunite with the body of the fleet; but, finding the English line so compact as to make this impracticable, she was obliged to abandon the attempt.

of a steam fleet, the penetration of the line by the enemy, if not entirely prevented, may be speedily reciprocated by tactical skill; for as a commander, by breaking the line of his opponent, divides his own line likewise, so, by a prompt movement, that part of the opponent's fleet which is not doubled upon, reversing simultaneously from its rear, may double upon that division of the fleet which had broken through the line attacked.

In the actions of sailing ships, great numbers of seamen are unavoidably withdrawn from the service of the guns, to attend to the sails, in order to preserve the proper distances between the ships in line ahead, for which it is necessary to keep the braces and bow-lines constantly *manned* ; and the most expert sailors are told off in squads denominated sail-trimmers, knotters, and splicers, for the performance of their several duties: the manœuvres of the sails, for the purpose of re-establishing order in changes of the wind, are, moreover, numerous and complicated, and Paul Hoste devotes a large portion of his work (pp. 68 to 79), and many diagrams, to an explanation of the manner of rectifying disorders which steam propulsion will entirely obviate. Steam-ships, having all their sails furled, permit the energies of the fighting crew to be wholly concentrated on the guns; the preservation of the distances and the movements of the ships being accomplished by the agency of the enginemen alone.

92. The importance of the windward position in the tactics of sailing ships, consists in the superior speed with which the ships, by sailing free, and therefore fast, may run rapidly down upon an enemy to leeward, and force him to fight, or abandon the field; but that advantage which the wind gives to a weather fleet, for this particular purpose, may be obtained, for every purpose, by a steam-fleet whose ships can put forth a greater degree of speed than those of the enemy.[a]

The amount of steam power for the propulsion of

---

[a] It may be said of well-commanded steam fleets, *mutato nomine*, as was said by an eminent tactician respecting manœuvring armies directed by generals of talent, that — " Entre deux armées pareilles ce sera enfin à qui l'emportera de génie et de *celerité* dans les manœuvres."—(*Guibert*, vol. ii. p. 187.)

ships of the line, during an action, should be limited to that which is barely sufficient to keep the ship under the guidance of the helm. Great steam-power occasions great and rapid movements, which are extremely unfavourable to good gunnery ; indeed, when engaged in close action with an enemy who is willing to fight, the ship should have as little motion as possible.

This steadiness is particularly necessary in receiving an attack from an enemy, on the beam, because his approach is, in that case, directly upon the broadside batteries of the ships attacked, and he is exposed to a fire so much the more destructive, as it is delivered from ships which are nearly at rest.

93. It does not follow that engines capable of putting forth great power, should be worked at high pressure, in ordinary evolutions. If the steam be cut off at any part of the stroke, so that that which has entered the cylinder may act expansively, the fuel is economized without any great loss of power. (See Arts. 8-10.) Even with the utmost economy in the consumption of fuel, screw steam-ships cannot in general, from a want of stowage-room for coals, continue more than a few days steaming either at full speed or expansively.[a] Exhaustion of fuel on the eve of a battle, or during a protracted action, is a contingency which must at all events be effectually guarded against.

94. Strategical combinations have not hitherto entered into the system of naval operations with sailing fleets, but are absolutely necessary with fleets of steamers. Sailing ships carry with them all the provisions and other supplies, by which they are enabled to keep the sea, and prosecute their service for periods of considerable duration ; but steam-ships, being dependent upon supplies of fuel, which must be, at short intervals, con-

---

[a] The average numbers of days steaming at full power, for which vessels of the under-mentioned classes can stow coal, are—

For ships of the 121 guns class	.. ..	8 days.
„ „ 90 guns, of the 'Renown' class	.. ..	6 „
„ „ 51 guns, of the 'Impérieuse' class..	..	8¾ „
„ „ 32 guns, of the 'Diadem' class	.. ..	6 „

The French type ship, the 'Napoleon,' has stowage sufficient for ten days' consumption at full speed, 12½ knots per hour.

stantly conveyed to the fleet from the ports where the depôts of coal have been formed, require the organization of a system of steam-transport, analogous to that which is established for keeping open the lines of communication between an army in the field and its base of operations.

But, however effectually this measure may provide for the evolutions of fleets under steam during an action, the want of an adequate supply of fuel renders it impossible that the strategical operations of fleets can be performed by steam alone ; and, on this account, it has been found necessary to provide steam-ships with full sailing, as well as with full steaming power.

95. The speed of the line-of-battle steamers serving in the same fleet should be as nearly as possible uniform ;[a]

[a] Horse-Power, Force, Dimensions, and Displacement of Ships of the Line, Screw-propelled.

Names.	Horse-Power.	Guns.	Length between Perpendiculars.	Breadth.	Displacement.
			Feet.		Tons.
Royal Sovereign	800	131	..	..	..
Royal Albert	500	130	232	60·83	5572
Marlborough	800	130	245	60·37	6100
Duke of Wellington	700	130	241	60·00	5680
Royal George	400	101	205	54·50	4814
Orion	600	91	238	55·75	..
Renown	800	91	245	55·75	4890
Revenge	800	91	245	55·33	,,
Atlas	800	91	245	55·75	,,
Anson	800	91	425	55·75	,,
Defiance	800	91	245	55·75	,,
Cæsar	400	91	208	56·00	not known
Algiers	600	91	219	60·00	,,
Agamemnon	600	91	230	55·42	,,
Exmouth	400	91	204	60·33	,,
Hannibal	450	91	218	60·00	,,
Princess Royal	400	91	217	58·10	4916
Cressy	400	80	199	55·00	3938
Majestic	400	80	190	57·00	not known
Goliath	400	80	190	56·75	,,
Meeanee	400	80	190	56·75	,,
Colossus	400	80	190	56.75	,,
Mars	400	80	190	56 75	,,
La Hogue	450	60	184	47·66	,,
Blenheim	450	60	181	47·66	,,

The speed of the 'Renown' is about 12 knots per hour, but there is a great inequality of speed in the line-of-battle steamers of the British navy.

if there are some ships in which the power of motion is greater than in others, they should be posted to the reserve, and employed to carry succour promptly wherever it may be required. The steam frigates and sloops attached to the fleet should be capable of exerting considerably more speed than the ships of the line, in order to enable them to be to the fleet what cavalry and horse-artillery are to an army.

If the steam-power of the several ships of the line forming a screw-fleet be not uniform, the speed of the whole fleet must be reduced to that of its slowest ship.[a] The serious inconvenience arising from an inequality of speed in the ships of a sailing fleet was felt by Lord Duncan in approaching the Dutch fleet off Camperdown, when a considerable time was lost in the attempt to close up and re-form the order of battle; the admiral being obliged to signal his good sailing ships to shorten sail, in order to enable the others to take their stations in line. There not being time to do this correctly, the British fleet was in a very disunited state at the commencement of the action. (James's 'Naval History,' vol. ii. p. 269.)

The fleet which, in anticipating the manœuvres of the enemy, or in manœuvring itself to get into action (perhaps on a flank of its opponent), can put forth the greatest steam-power, possesses a decided advantage over the other, for which no tactical skill on the part of its commander can compensate.[b] In the formation of the steam navy of Great Britain this subject, which is

---

[a] It appears from the preceding Table that great discrepancies exist in the amounts of horse-power exerted by the engines compared with the gunnery force and the displacements of the ships; and it is evident that, if these ships were combined in one fleet, the more powerful steamers would be retarded in their progress by the necessity of keeping in company with the others: hence the whole fleet would be deficient in that most important quality—celerity of movement.

[b] "La rapidité d'un batiment à hélice étant un des principaux éléments de sa puissance militaire, tous les fourneaux sont allumés en présence de l'ennemi, et les feux prêts à être poussés au premier signal ou au moment favorable."— *Ministère de la Marine et des Colonies:*—'Instructions Officielles sur la Tactique Navale,' Art. II., p. 49.

one of the utmost importance, has not, apparently, been
duly considered; and there is reason to believe that
the general speed of a large fleet of French steamers is
superior to that of a British fleet consisting of an equal
number of ships.   We have the testimony of Admiral
De la Gravière to the importance which the French
naval officers attach to superior swiftness in sailing
ships and steamers, in the subjoined quotation from his
work, entitled ' Guerres Maritimes.' [a]

96. The operation of changing the direction of the
front, by a movement on the centre, is highly objectionable with a fleet of steamers; since, in throwing back
a wing, the movement must be effected either by backing the steamers or by reversing (countermarching)
them.   The first of these methods is inexpedient, whilst
the other is extremely difficult to perform in good
order, and is likely to produce confusion, of which
an intelligent enemy will not fail to take advantage
It follows that the measure of placing the slowest
going ships in the centre of the line, and the fastest
on the flanks, on the ground that the flank ships
have the greatest distances to pass over, is not to be
recommended.   A change of direction should be made
by wheeling on a flank ship as a moving pivot.

97. All tactical evolutions of fleets consisting wholly
of steamers, or of these in combination with ships provided both with steam and sails, should be made under
steam exclusively; since the employment of steam propulsion in some only of the ships would necessarily
subject the whole to all the limitations imposed by the
wind.   The tactics of steam-fleets constitute a new art
which is capable of producing great effects; but if these
are combined with the tactics of sailing fleets, the

---

[a] " La marche du navire, ne l'oublions pas, est la condition *essentielle* pour
une marine exposée à trouver toujours l'ennemi en nombre.
    " La vitesse du navire étant admise comme un des gages les plus certains de
succès, tout navire à voiles ou à vapeur, qu'il en fût à son débût ou à son
vingtième armement, devrait, en sortant du port, être appelé à faire ses
preuves de vitesse devant une commission qui pût le comparer à un batiment
de la flotte dont les qualités seraient incontestables."—De la Gravière,
' Guerres Maritimes,' tom. ii. pp. 278, 279.

peculiar advantages of steam propulsion will be wholly, or in a great measure, neutralized.

98. The vitality of a screw steam-ship with its sails furled, will depend entirely upon the unimpaired efficiency of its machinery; but the liability of a screw to be broken or fouled, by spars, ropes, or other materials, is a very serious contingency, which in a battle is very likely to occur (see Art. 75). The deeds to be accomplished by colossal fleets will depend upon the efficiency of the screw, just as the success of the bombardment of a fortress depends upon the fuzes of shells duly performing their office; and the failure of a screw may defeat the execution of a great naval operation, should such an accident happen to any of the ships of a steam-fleet, when keeping a course upon which the sails cannot act; for unless the course of the fleet be changed to that on which the sails of the ships with disabled screws can receive the impulse of the wind, these last must be captured : such a combination of the moving powers wind and steam is, however, subject to the disadvantages alluded to in the preceding article.

99. Since, for the reasons stated in Art. 93, the use of sails cannot, in steam fleets, be at present dispensed with, it will still be prudent, in steam warfare, to continue the practice of firing at the masts and rigging of an enemy's ship, before coming to close action, with a view of dismantling the rigging and of increasing the probability of disabling the screw by the falling spars and fragments of sails and ropes becoming entangled with it; after this every shot should be made to tell upon the hull.

The battle over, the fleet must, or should, pass from steaming to sailing, in order to economize fuel, which may be wholly or nearly exhausted during the action; the like expenditure of fuel may have taken place in the enemy's fleet, and this, together with the dismantling effects produced upon the rigging of his ships, will impede or prevent his escape. Both sailing and steaming power, in the same ship, must therefore

be always kept in a state of efficiency. In the early
days of steam propulsion, it was imagined by Paixhans
and others, that a few small steamers, with little or no
sailing power, might destroy or capture any ship if
properly attacked on her weak points; and this is true
in calms, and of operations in inland seas and waters,
in which fleets of large ships of war can neither
manœuvre, nor follow vessels of small draught of water
into shallow creeks or channels. But for steam-warfare
on the ocean, ships must be rigged and equipped with
full sailing power, and, consequently, fully manned with
able seamen as before; and thus, nautical skill and good
practical seamanship will be as necessary as ever to
steam-fleets, and will continue to tell, as heretofore, in
favour of that party which is most proficient in nautical
skill and expert seamanship. It must not therefore be
assumed, in preparing for steam-warfare, that the sail
will be entirely supplanted by steam, or that steam
fleets may dispense with crews of able seamen.

100. A smooth sea and no wind is always propitious
for steaming and for good gunnery; but, in a perfect
calm, contending fleets would be enveloped in such
dense clouds of vapour and smoke that neither the
ships nor the signals of the chiefs could be seen; this disadvantage is felt even when a gentle breeze is blowing;
and, in this case, it is more or less favourable or unfavourable to either fleet according as it may be placed
with respect to the direction of the wind.— (Paul Hoste,
Translated by Capt. Boswall, R.N., pp. 23 to 27.)

The direction and force of the wind, and thereby
the setting and amount of the swell, though immaterial
to the progress of steam-ships, are important disturb-
ances to the practice of gunnery. With the swell
abeam, or a cross-swell, the rolling motion of a heavily-
masted steam-ship with the sails furled, will be far
greater and more rapid than it would be when those
motions are checked by sails. The gunnery of a steam
fleet, will not, therefore, excepting in a smooth sea, be
so efficient as that of a fleet of sailing ships; and it
will require all the skill and tact of well-trained seamen-

gunners, to watch the roll and catch the proper moment of pulling the trigger-line. See Naval Gunnery, 4th ed., Art. 383, *et seq.*

101. The movements of steam fleets may, like those of armies, be conducted on tactical principles best adapted to the great end of all preliminary manœuvres —the formation for battle in the most simple, speedy, and precise manner. This power of executing the evolutions of fleets and armies on the same tactical principles, cannot but be considered as one of the greatest benefits which will result from the application of steam propulsion in naval warfare.

The intended formation may, in all cases, be accomplished by steam-fleets, with as much precision as the formation of an army on land, and with the like regard to the avoidance of a premature display of the whole force, or a disclosure of the intentions of the commander.[a]

102. This avoidance is seldom possible with fleets of sailing ships : the complicated manœuvres, and the time required to execute the formation of columns, or divisions, of ships into one long line of battle in presence of an enemy, particularly if he be to windward, are such, that, fearful of being attacked while the evolutions are being made, fleets of sailing ships are generally extended into line, before it is tactically prudent, or, with steamers, necessary to do so.[b]

103. In exemplification of the complexity of the evolutions required in forming a line of battle, let it be supposed that a fleet, sailing upon a wind in three parallel columns, each in line ahead, is signalled to form line upon the centre column—and this is a forma-

---

[a] " Un général habile et tacticien, s'il est dans la nécessité de recevoir une bataille, ne démasquera sa disposition de défense qu'après qu'il aura reconnu les points où l'ennemi veut faire effort. Il tiendra son armée en colonnes sur le champ de bataille qu'il devra occuper, afin de ne déterminer la repartition de ses troupes que sur celle des troupes de l'ennemi."—(*Guibert*, vol. ii. p. 185.)

[b] Numerous instances of the difficulty, uncertainty, and the time required to form sailing ships into line of battle, may be met with in naval history. In the action between the British and French fleets in the East Indies, in 1782, Sir Edward Hughes, seeing that Admiral Suffrein was bearing down upon him, made the signal at daylight to form line ahead, but, on account of the variable state of the wind, the line could not be formed before eight o'clock.

tion which can be more rapidly executed than one upon either of the other columns—the windward division bears down and forms line ahead of the central division; the ships of the lee division tack, simultaneously, and stand on, till they fetch into the wake of the division to be formed upon; and then, tacking again, proceed as quickly as possible to close to their stations in the new line. If the formation is to be made on the windward division, the process is still more complicated and protracted : both the centre and rear divisions tack simultaneously, and, when they have *fetched*, in succession, into the wake of the windward division, tack again, and close to their stations in the new line ; thus having to make two tacks and two " *boards;*" passing therefore over two sides of a triangle instead of one, and being at the same time subject to the contingencies of the wind. In steam fleets this operation may be simply executed by its ships proceeding rapidly and with certainty in diagonal lines to take their proper places.

104. These and all other formations may be executed with so much certainty and celerity by steam fleets at any time, that the practice of extending ships into line, and particularly into a single line of battle, as soon as, or even before, the fleets come into the presence of each other, will be renounced in naval, as it has long since been in military, tactics. Well-exercised steam-fleets, like well-trained armies in the field, if skilfully commanded, should be kept concentrated in columns, or lines of bearing *en échelon,* so disposed as to be under the eye of the commander, and within good signalling distance, ever ready to execute the movements which he may order.

105. Modern military science renounces the practice of fighting in parallel order, line against line, multitude against multitude, ignorance against chance; and it substitutes for that rude and primitive formation, the more skilful and less sanguinary methods which were practised with splendid success during the Seven Years' War, and have since been almost invariably adopted. This method consists in turning the enemy's

flank by an·oblique movement, in attacking him while on a march; or, by tactical combinations, bringing a vastly superior force upon the point attacked.[a]

Naval officers of the old school, when ships were the slaves of the wind, may at first sight be disposed to repudiate, perhaps to ridicule, the adoption in their profession, of the principles of military movements and formations, as recommended and expounded by the author. But moved as fleets will hereafter be by the obedient agency of steam, so that the station of each ship in a fleet, and the time to be occupied in performing any evolution, can be determined with as much exactness as the post of a regiment or brigade in an army, and the time required to arrive at it; it must follow that the evolutions of ships of war will be susceptible of being executed with a precision hitherto unknown in the naval service.

A distinguished and skilful admiral in the British navy has not only anticipated but met a total change in our naval tactics in this respect, and has recognised the military character which naval operations will assume from the introduction of steam propulsion. In a tract published by Admiral Bowles, C.B., in 1846,[b] that gallant officer observed, that we had then arrived at a new era, in which steam would enable naval commanders to conduct their operations and manœuvres on military and scientific principles; that fleets, moving by a force beyond the influence of wind and weather, would have it in their power to attack, or repulse an enemy in a manner hitherto unknown in naval actions; that an admiral by keeping his ships together in a collected and manageable order, and skilfully manœuvred, could prevent the recurrence of the many indecisive and unsuccessful naval engagements of times past; and he

---

[a] Thus Frederick II. defeated the French army at Rossbach with the loss of only 500 men, killed and wounded, while the French loss amounted to 3000 men, killed and wounded, and 5000 taken prisoners. Thus also, Napoleon I. defeated the combined Austrian and Russian armies at Austerlitz.—(See also *Guibert*, vol. ii. p. 187.)

[b] 'Essay on Naval Tactics,' Ridgway, 1846.

concludes that very able tract, by observing that, as in an army, so in a fleet, the force would be handled in such way as to bring the fleet into action so as to enable it to exert its powers with the most decisive advantage. To this high authority may be added that of Captain Dahlgren, U. S. Navy,[a] who observes that the principles of military tactics will, hereafter, enter largely into the manœuvres of fleets.

106. The rude practice of forming a fleet for battle in one long line, has hitherto prevailed in naval warfare on account, chiefly, of the difficulties and uncertainties imposed by the wind, in executing compound evolutions with sailing ships. These difficulties will not exist for fleets consisting wholly of steam-ships. Armies in the field move in as many columns as there may be practicable roads, or opened routes leading to the point at which the intended deployment in order of battle is to take place ; but at sea a steam fleet may always be moved in as many columns as there are divisions in its formation, and each ship of a fleet may be considered as corresponding to a battalion in a land army.

107. There is this difference, however :— a fleet in line ahead, moving parallel to an enemy's line, is making a flank movement, and is at the same time in line of battle, which is not the case with an army making a flank movement. A fleet in line abreast is in an important order of steaming ; and though it is not, properly speaking, in order of battle, yet ships in that position may commence action, each with the fire of seven or nine powerful bow-guns, and are quite in readiness to form *échelon of ships* or *line ahead*, for offensive or defensive measures, as the case may require, by a simple movement of each ship.

108. The columns of a steam fleet should be arranged in two lines of bearing, making with each other an angle of 8 points, or 90° ; the lines being formed on a central ship, which is commonly distinguished by the flag of a divisional admiral or other squadron officer. The flag-

---

[a] 'Shells and Shell-guns,' p. 394.

ship of the admiral commanding in chief is posted as usual in the centre of his fleet, unless he should quit that position and take post at the head of either squadron, the better to superintend and direct the execution of his plans of operation. In so doing, be it observed, he ought not to supersede the divisional officer commanding the squadron to which he may repair ; for, in no case, should the commander-in-chief be burthened with the details of any divisional movements. The position which the flag-ship before occupied is to be supplied by a ship of the line placed behind the admiral's flag-ship, and bearing the same number ; this is called the duplicate or substitute vessel, being a substitute for that of the admiral, and distinguished by the divisional flag of the squadron to which she belongs.[a]

109. A fleet steaming in divisions, each formed in a double column of ships in lines of bearing, having its advanced posts of steam sloops, with supports of steam frigates, considerably in advance, and a reserve of swift ships of the line (Fig. 8, p. 92), possesses great military strength, from the reciprocal defence which the ships afford to each other, as shown by the lines of fire (figs. 13 and 14, p. 98), and could not be broken in upon by an enemy without severe loss and much danger to himself. This order of steaming is moreover admirably calculated to take immediate advantage of any error or false movement on the part of the enemy, by the prompt convertibility of the columns severally into lines *en échelon*, and the formation of the whole into order of battle in any direction.

Line may be formed in the direction A B (fig. 8), by bringing up the heads of the three columns, *l, n, p,* into that alignment, and then forming them into lines on their respective centre ships ; or, should an enemy appear on the starboard or N.E. quarter, the left column (*l*) should be brought up to *m* and the whole form échelon

---

[a] This is now the French practice.—(*Batailles de Mer*, par l'Amiral Comte Bouet Willaumetz, p. 421 ; fig. 48, p. 423.) It would be preferable to call up a line-of-battle ship from the reserve, to serve as the substitute ship.

of divisions in line, by moving up the port branches of
each double column into line with their respective
starboard branches, and so be in a position either to

Fig. 8.

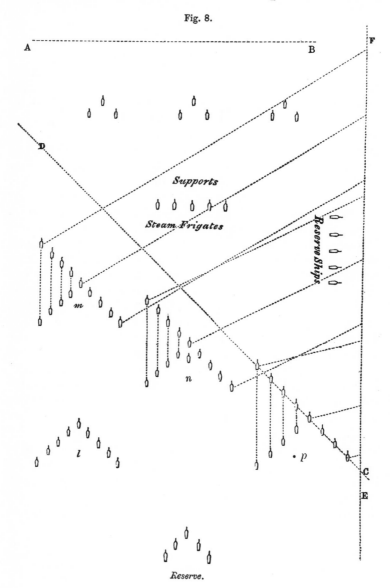

Reserve.

form line in the direction C D, or by changing the courses of ships to the N.E., form line to the right in the direction E F. In like manner the fleet may form line to the left, or port, should the appearance of the enemy be in that quarter.

110. Columns of ships in performing evolutions to be followed by formations on a front line, as with armies, should have little depth, in order that the line may be formed as speedily as possible. Now columns of ships ranged in line ahead cannot be closer in file than, at least, one cable's length (720 feet), without the risk of getting foul of one another; and assuming each ship to be 250 feet long, a squadron of 7 ships in a double column, line ahead formed on a centre ship, as in fig. 9, would occupy in depth above 1050 yards; while the same number of ships, if formed in a double column, in lines of bearing,[a] as in fig. 10, would only extend in depth 330 yards.

Fig. 9.

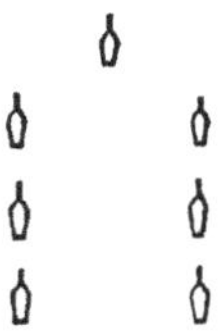

Fig. 10.

111. The order of sailing in line of bearing is, perhaps, by the reciprocal defence which the ships afford each other, that alone which can properly be considered as founded on sound tactical principles. But this order is, with sailing ships, restricted to particular cases, being dependent on the wind, and is with difficulty retained; while, by the agency of steam, the oblique order[b] and échelon formations are at all times possible and easily put in practice, and should be generally used not only in orders of movement, but in

---

[a] Lines of bearing, when the ships are disposed en échelon, are commonly called by seamen *bow and quarter* lines; because, by the obliquity of the ships to the general line of their direction, the bow and the quarter of each ship are brought respectively opposite the quarter and bow of that which is nearest to it.

[b] "L'ordre oblique est l'ordre de bataille le plus usité, le plus savant, et le plus susceptible de combinaisons."—(*Guibert*, vol. ii. p. 73.) This is said of armies on land; and the same may be predicated of steam fleets in oblique and échelon formations at sea.—(See *Batailles de Terre et de Mer*, by M. Bouet de Willaumetz, p. 425.)

anchoring the ships of a fleet in line of bearing athwart
the wind or the tide, so that no ship can drive on the
hawse of another. Those orders, and the movements
arising from them, will therefore, no doubt, be henceforth generally used in naval warfare between steam
fleets.

112. In the tactics of sailing fleets the lines of bearing
were confined to the two close-hauled lines, in either
of which the ships might be ranged in line ahead, or
en échelon, on the same tack, at six points from the
wind. Thus the ships might be in line ahead, as at
A B (fig. 11), or on the same tack (starboard) in the

Fig. 11.

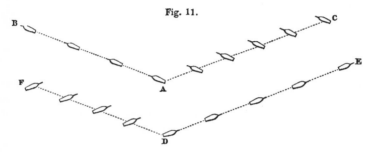

line of bearing A C; or they might be in line ahead,
as at D E, or on the same tack (port) in the line of
bearing D F. From either of these positions the whole
may be formed in order of battle on either tack, by
causing the ships en échelon, A C, D F, to form line, in
rear of A B or D E.

But no movement to windward of the close-hauled
lines could be made by sailing ships, except by the slow
process of tacking and *fetching-up* against the wind;
therefore, within the space contained between the two
close-hauled lines, forming with each other an angle
equal to 12 points of the compass or 135°, sailing ships
have not the power of making any direct attack upon,
or any movement towards, the enemy.

113. A fleet ranged thus might sail, with the wind.
suppose at north, on any course from E.N.E. round by
the south, and from thence haul up to W.N.W.; but

here the use of the sail ceases, and that of steam propulsion continues or may commence. Steam ships can
manœuvre in any direction, in calms, and up to the
wind's eye; and a well-constituted and skilfully-commanded steam fleet might, by acting in the space, or
on courses where a sailing fleet cannot manœuvre, sink,
burn, or capture the ships of such a fleet even of far
superior force.

114. The order of retreat before the wind, on two
lines of bearing, making with each other an angle of
135°, is represented in fig. 12, from which it may

Fig. 12.

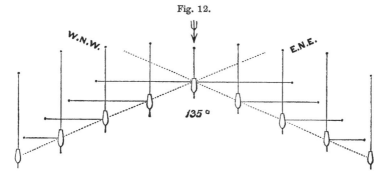

be seen, by the lines of fire, how the ships defend each
other towards the rear, reciprocally, and check the
enemy's pursuit by the fires of their respective stern
batteries; and likewise how strong this order is on
both flanks by the crossing of the stern fires with both
the broadside batteries of the ship at the angle, and
with the outward broadsides fires of all the other ships
in this order.

The invention of this order of retreat has been erro-
neously stated to be of very recent date; but the
reader will find that it is fully described by Paul Hoste
in his Treatise (p. 42, Captain Boswall's Translation),
as that which was practised by Van Tromp in the naval
combat off Portland in 1653. The retreat of Admiral
Cornwallis, in 1796, was also conducted on this principle. (James, vol. i. p. 240.)

115. Paul Hoste, sensible that the order of sailing

in two lines of bearing forming with each other an angle of 135°, is too extended, states that the wings should be brought closer together: this observation is just, and may be acted on with a fleet of steamers. With a sailing fleet it would be impossible without abandoning the principle on which the order of retreat is founded; an adherence to which is indispensable for a sailing fleet, in order, as has been said, that the ships in either wing may form line of battle ahead, simply by *hauling-up* on the starboard or port-tack, as the case may be.

In a fleet of steamers, it were better that the angle between the two lines of bearing should be not greater than one of 90°; it might even be less, except for that case in which a convoy is to be protected between the wings, as in Van Tromp's retreat above referred to.

116. Sailing ships are so liable to be dismantled in their rigging and sails; and such is the difficulty of regulating their speed when sailing *free*, by *bracing by* or other complicated manipulations of the sail, that these nice and delicate formations could not be precisely executed, and therefore were rarely attempted.[a]

The ships of a fleet sailing in line of bearing will, with great difficulty, maintain their positions with respect to each other,[b] and will be very likely thrown into confusion; but this order may be preserved with the utmost precision by steam fleets moving on lines of bearing; and, with great facility, the courses may be changed into directions perpendicular or oblique to

---

[a] Few instances can be found in the naval history of the war arising out of the great French Revolution, in which the formation of a fleet in line of bearing was practised in presence of the enemy, on account of the difficulty of manœuvring the sailing ships. On the 31st May, 1794, Lord Howe, having made the signal for the ships of his fleet to come to the wind together on the larboard tack, soon afterwards made the signal to form the larboard line of bearing; and in this order he edged down towards the enemy for the purpose of engaging his van, centre, and rear at the same time; but many of the British ships, being slow sailers, fell so far astern that, although a general action might have been brought on that evening had there been no slow ships, the British Admiral was obliged to postpone the battle to the next day.

[b] Paul Hoste, 'Naval Tactics,' translated by Captain Boswall, R.N., ch. 8.

such lines. Steam fleets and squadrons of evolution should be often exercised in these movements, since such will undoubtedly be of frequent occurrence, and will have to be executed with the utmost precision, in the event of a war taking place;[a] and the subject deserves, therefore, the attentive consideration of the naval administration in this country. The large fleets that were employed in the Baltic, and in the Black Sea during the late war, being engaged in particular services, which were rather of a military than of a naval character, it was impossible for them to practise steam evolutions, even if the fleets had been entirely composed of steam ships, which was far from being the case.

117. The defensive order of sailing in double échelon, which, in the tactics of sailing fleets, could only be used to cover the retreat of a fleet sailing free, or before the wind, may, with a steam fleet, be converted into an offensive formation resembling the work called a redan in field fortifications ; and such a disposition of the ships may be applied in advance of a naval line of battle with great advantage.

118. In land formations a simple redan is extremely defective ; without flanks the sectoral space before its salient angle is undefended, and its faces are unprotected by collateral fires. But the formation in a double échelon, consisting of 3, 5, or any other uneven number of ships, like a redan with parapets *en cremaillère*, has, on the contrary, great strength. The space before the salient angle A (figs. 13 and 14, p. 98) is defended by the fire of the powerful bow-guns of all the ships in the formation, whilst both broadsides of the ship at A, together with the outside broadside batteries of the ships in both wings, defend the heads of the ships next astern.

When this angular formation is applied in front of, and to strengthen the positions of fleets, as redans are,

---

" Cet ordre (en échelon) est difficile à observer, mais il est utile de le rendre familier aux vaisseaux d'une flotte à vapeur, lesquels seront appelées à le pratiquer dans les évolutions navales."—(Bouet de Willaumetz, *Batailles dè Mer.*)

in military defences, to strengthen other works, the
salient angle need not be greater than 60°, or a little

Fig. 13.

Fig. 14.

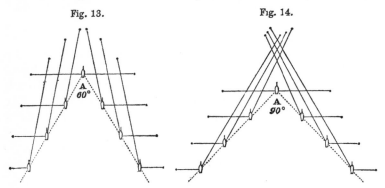

more than 5½ points of the compass, as in fig. 13.   But
when applied to the formation of double columns in the
movements of fleets, as shown in fig. 8, p. 92, the salient
angle should contain 8 points (a right angle), as in
fig. 14, the better to provide for the military strength
of that order of steaming, by the flanked and flanking
branches of the double columns (as the right of *n* and
the left of *p*, fig. 8) being perpendicular to each other.

119. The French are good theoretical tacticians and
skilful practitioners of the modern science of war ; and
if Guibert's essay on the Tactics of Armies be denominated the best commentary that has appeared
on the tactics of land armies, it may with equal truth
be said that Paul Hoste's treatise of Naval Warfare is
the root from which all subsequent writings on that
subject have sprung.   Now the celerity and precision
with which steam fleets may execute any evolutions
whatever will, hereafter, allow the principles of tactics
on land to be applied to the movements of ships on the
ocean, with this advantage on the side of the naval
operations, that the inequalities of ground, which so
seriously embarrass the manœuvres of troops, do not
exist at sea.   The author, therefore, proposes to estab-
lish the analogy between the tactics of armies in the
field, and those of steam fleets on the ocean, with the

view of drawing from that analogy such lessons as may be found useful in naval warfare.

120. An eminent military tactician has well said that the art of fortification and that of field tactics are intimately connected with each other (Guibert, vol. ii., p. 194); and that the latter derives many of its principles from the art of constructing permanent for-tresses. In both, the important object is to dispose the parts, whether works or bodies of troops, so that they may mutually protect each other; and he infers that, to be a good tactician in the field, a knowledge of military engineering is necessary. Of a good naval tactician it may be said, in like manner, that he should so dispose the ships of a fleet that they may mutually protect one another.

Reciprocal defence is obtained in the construction of military works by breaking the line of front into angular formations, so as to permit some of the parts to defend others by lines of fire parallel, or nearly so, to these last, and reciprocally to be defended in a similar manner by the others. There is no difficulty in apply-ing this principle to naval formations, since, whatever be the order of steaming, the ships must always be parallel to each other; and it is only necessary, there-fore, to place some of the ships en échelon on each flank, as shown at C D and E F, fig. 15.

Fig. 15.

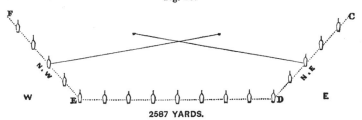

2587 YARDS.

Ranged in this order, a powerful defence is obtained by the broadside fire of the ships en echelon on either wing, and by the crossing fire from the bows of the ships in line abreast. When the enemy approaches near the fleet, the order of the main body, E D, should be changed into line ahead, a movement analogous to the deployment of columns of troops into line of battle: the ships in this order may then use their broadside batteries, as the deployed line of troops would use its direct fire; while the body of the fleet will be powerfully protected by the crossing fires from the bow and stern batteries of the ships in the wings, as the line of troops would be protected by the batteries on its flanks.

121. As the formation of the line of battle en échelon, offensive or defensive, may appear at first sight difficult of execution, and even to be not admissible, it is proposed here to examine minutely the conditions of the case; and the author trusts that he shall be able to show that the manœuvre is easy with a fleet of steam ships, and that it has great advantages over the formation in line ahead.

1. Steam ships may preserve the échelon order with great facility and precision, since the manœuvre will depend only on keeping, by the compass,[a] all the ships on the same line of bearing and on the same course; and this can be done even at night, or when the ships are enveloped in smoke : the lofty masts of the adjacent ships will always be guides by which to keep in the échelon position.

Fig. 16.

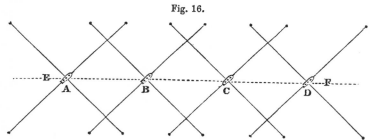

2. Ships so ranged are in no danger of being fired into by those on their right or left. For let the four ships A, B, C, D, fig. 16, be considered as a portion of a

---

[a] As the compasses in the different ships may differ from one another on account of the variable action of the iron in the ship on the needle, or from other causes, it is evident that the compasses in the ships should be often compared together by signal, and, if necessary, corrected.

fleet in the line of bearing E F, east and west, while
the ships are steaming on N.E. courses, the intervals
between the ships being 970 feet, measuring from the
centre of one ship to that of the next in the line ;[a] then
the direct fire from the bow guns of either ship will
cross the fire from the midship broadside guns of the
next ship on the bow, at not less than 420 feet from
each ship, even if that fire be perpendicular to her
course.   The bow-guns of ships ranged in this order
should fire only solid shot, in order to avoid any risk of
injury from the splinters of shells that may break in the
guns.   Shells may, however, be fired from the outward
broadside batteries of ships, provided, to avoid the
risk of injuring the nearest ships, the guns are trained
so as to fire before the beam.

3. Every line-of-battle ship carries on each of her
fighting decks, and on her forecastle, two bow guns,
which cannot be used in line of battle ahead ; while, in
the échelon order of battle, the guns on the starboard
bow, together with all those on the port bow, which
cannot take part in broadside action, would be of
efficient use in increasing the gunnery power of the ship.[b]

Ships steaming in this order, not being in the wake of
each other, cannot get foul either by drawing ahead or
lagging astern, and would, therefore, avoid any wrecks
of ropes, spars, or sails, shot away from other ships,
which, if in line ahead, would drift into the courses of
the ships astern and foul their screws.   Each ship
should, it is obvious, take as much care as possible to
prevent its screw from being fouled by the wrecks of
its own rigging, by keeping them, as much as possible,
in-board, or, at least, out of its wake.

---

[a] This distance is given on the supposition that the distance between two
ships in line ahead is 720 feet, a cable's length, measuring from the head of
one to the stern of the next in front, to which is added half the length of each
of two nearest ships, considered as equal to 125 feet : thus making up the
space between the centres of every two ships in the line ahead.

[b] In a fleet consisting of twenty sail of the line, two-deckers, the bow guns
which may thus be brought into action may amount to 180.   If there are any
three-deckers in the fleet, the efficient bow guns may amount to even a greater
number.

122. A number of ships disposed en échelon on any line of bearing may, therefore, be assimilated to a chain of redoubts, or a line of entrenchment *en cremaillère*, or to bodies of infantry in squares, with diagonals parallel to the front; and may thus, by means of their bow-guns and their broadside batteries, defend each other reciprocally—the stronger points of one ship defending the weaker points of another, as in fig. 15 above, and in fig. 18, p. 106.

123. Small steamers armed at the bow and stern should always act in pairs, whether for attack or defence. So associated, two vessels, with less expenditure in men and material, will, by the reciprocal defence which they may afford each other, and by their power of rapidly changing their positions as circumstances may require, be more formidable than one ship which is double the size of either, and, if well managed, they would be an overmatch for such a ship.

124. A line-of-battle ship fully armed at bow and stern, as well as on her broadsides, has no dead points, since she can bring guns to bear in every direction about her. The bows of such ships are armed with a 68-pounder solid-shot pivot-gun, and there are, besides, four bow guns on each deck. The trunk, or aperture through which the screw is hoisted up in order to be repaired or replaced (Art. 60), interferes with the armament of line-of-battle ships, where the free use of two guns on each deck is, on this account, greatly impeded; consequently there may be said to be only two stern guns on each deck which are wholly effective.[a] Thus the bow batteries of a two-decked ship consist of nine heavy guns, and those of a three-decked ship of eleven. The stern batteries of a two and a three decked ship consist, respectively, of four guns and six guns at least. Though ships of the line are thus really strong at bow and stern, these are technically called the weak points when compared with the superior strength of the

---

[a] The trunk does not interfere with the pivot guns of frigates and flush-deck vessels, the shutters of the trunk forming the deck over it. See also Art. 79, p. 67.

broadside batteries, which are therefore denominated the strong points.

125. When a fleet of ships is thrown into échelon, the bow-batteries are brought into play, and it is of the first importance that they should be as strong as possible. In the disposition shown in fig. 16, the pivot gun should be established on the port fighting point, and the unoccupied bow ports on each deck should be armed with the nearest guns, shifted into them from the starboard broadside batteries, where they are useless. All the broadside guns on the fighting side should be trained to fire as much before the beam as the width of the ports will permit, and this, with respect to the midship guns, is at an angle of 37° 30', as shown in figure 17,[a] but the angle is less in the after ports, on account of the tapering form of the ship towards the stern. The reason for thus training the guns is, obviously, that their fire upon the enemy's ships may be less oblique, may reach him at shorter ranges, and be wider of the bows of the next following ship.

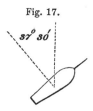

Fig. 17.

When a fleet is ranged in order of battle called line ahead, not only is there no reciprocal defence, but a great amount of gunnery power in the bow-batteries is utterly out of action; this, in a fleet of twenty ships of the line, of which six may be three-deckers, will amount to 152 heavy guns, whose fire is masked by the leading ships.

The inartificial practice of forming a fleet for battle in one line of great extent, in which the ships are devoid of the power of protecting each other by reciprocal defence, and without a second line as a reserve, ought now to be abandoned, as a corresponding practice with armies in the field has been renounced in warfare on land.

126. Freed from the caprices of the wind and from the

---

[a] Great Gun Exercise, 'Excellent,' p. 46.

complicated manœuvres of the sail, the movements of
steam fleets will no longer be limited to any particular
line of bearing, nor to one order of battle, in line ahead,
in any particular direction ; and the national interests
will no longer be staked on the risks of a battle fought
in that unskilful position ; that is upon the chance of
being able to prevent a line everywhere weak from
being penetrated or doubled upon.

127. In the échelon formation the broadside fires of all
the ships may be made to cross upon an enemy, whether
attacking or attacked. If the obliquity of the ships to
the line of bearing be less than forty-five degrees, the
flanking fires from the bow-guns will be too close to
the vessel flanked to be safe ; if greater, they will be too
open. It follows that the angle which the keel of each
ship should make with the line of bearing, should be
equal to half a right angle ; and it may be remarked
that every shot from a broadside, which takes effect, is
fired directly from a ship, but is received obliquely on
that of the enemy advancing perpendicularly to the line
of bearing, and is, therefore, to a certain extent, a raking
fire.

128. A consideration of the figure (fig. 16, p. 100) will
make it evident that if the rear of the fleet were attacked
on the starboard quarter, the échelon formation would
afford the advantages of a reciprocal fire from 4 or 8 stern
guns of each ship, and the starboard broadside batteries
of the ships on its left. Since, therefore, every ship has
both its broadsides and its end-on fires open, it is plain
that a fleet steaming in this order has a vast degree
of military strength, and is therefore in a good order of
advance or of retreat : it has, besides, the advantage of
lending itself easily to any ulterior evolutions.

129. Notwithstanding the great gunnery power which
ships of the line possess, they, as well as other ships,
are subject to such great disadvantages when exposed
to an enfilading or raking fire, that an end-on position
in action should be avoided as much as possible. But
if the ships of a fleet are arranged in échelon order, the
exposure is of little moment ; since, as may be seen in

the figure, should the enemy attempt to take advantage of that position to enfilade the ships, he must necessarily put his own ships in the like order, in which position they are themselves liable to be enfiladed, and thus, *cæteris paribus*, the action would be continued on equal terms.

There may, perhaps, be a lingering prejudice against this novel formation for action, on the alleged ground that it is entirely theoretical. To this the author would reply that such a formation is not novel in principle, and has been often practised even with the sail, as appears by the well-known order of retreat (see fig. 12, p. 95), each wing of which, taken singly, is, in fact, an échelon formation, exactly conformable to the formation of a fleet in line of bearing, as shown in fig. 16. The order of retreat is strong on both flanks, by the reciprocal fire of the ships which compose it ; and it is strong in rear, by the fire of the *stern* and broadside batteries crossing each other. It cannot by sailing ships be reversed so as to form an order of advance ; but by steam propulsion this may be done ; in which case the broadside and bow-batteries of the ships will respectively cross each other. Unless, then, it can be shown, by any who demur to the author's proposition, that the order of retreat which has so frequently been practised, successfully, by fleets of sailing ships, is unsound in principle, and so restricted in its application as not to be practicable on all occasions ; it must follow that the proposed order of battle, in which the ships are ranged en échelon, is one of great strength and convenience. It may indeed be executed by steam fleets on any lines of bearing with the utmost precision and certainty ; and there can be no doubt that this formation will become of extensive use in the tactics of steam fleets.

An advantage of perhaps vital importance results from ranging ships for action in this oblique order. The sterns of steam ships, which, by the propinquity of the moving and steering powers, must be considered their most vulnerable parts, are screened from the fire of the enemy's ships, instead of being exposed to it. If formed in line ahead, the ships are exposed to a cannon-

H

ade aimed at their sterns, which, if it take effect between
the inner and outer sternposts, in which space are
imbedded the rudder-head and case, the trunk, the
yoke, and other steering apparatus, it might reduce a
formidable steam ship into a very helpless and impotent
antagonist.

130. A fleet, consisting of nine ships of the line,
ranged in line abreast in the centre, and en échelon
on the wings (fig. 15), at the distance of 970 feet
from each other, measured from centre to centre, will
cover a space of nearly 2600 yards, in which case the
fire of the ships en échelon on each flank will cross
each other efficiently in front of the ships in line;
but a fleet consisting of 20 sail of the line or upwards
should put forward an uneven number of its ships, say
5 or 7, and form them in double échelon on the centre,
as in fig. 18, disposing them so that their fire in both

Fig. 18.

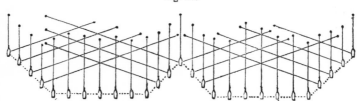

directions may cross the fires from the two wings. This
formation resembles very much a front of fortification,
and, like such a front, it possesses great military
strength.

It must be understood, however, that this disposition
of ships in a fleet, and also that described in Art. 120,
are consistent chiefly with the occupation of purely
defensive positions, in circumstances which make it
impossible, or at least difficult, for the enemy by *turning*
either wing of the fleet, to avoid attacking it in front:
this may be the case when it is required to defend a
strait of the sea. If the position be on the wide ocean,
and the enemy, declining to attack in front the fleet
which is on the defensive, should move towards a flank

with a view of turning it; the ships en échelon may
speedily be moved into the general line, and the whole
fleet may change its position, moving in line towards
the menaced side.   In doing this, it will have to
describe only the *chord*, while the enemy's fleet will
have to pass over the length of the *arc*; the commander
of the fleet on the defensive will, therefore, be able to
anticipate his opponent, and, probably, to frustrate his
intention.

131. Fleets of sailing ships have ever had their
look-out frigates and small vessels in attendance for the
purpose of obtaining intelligence; but such vessels have
not been used as advanced guards to cover the fleet, on
account of the impossibility of keeping such ships out
of the lines of fire from the fleet; but with steam fleets
it will be practicable, and highly important, to adopt
in this respect a practice corresponding to that of an
army in an open country, by having advanced posts
of small and swift steamers, with supports composed
of steam frigates, (fig. 8, p. 92), so that an enemy may
not be able to approach without driving back these
advanced posts, and thus, in some degree, disclosing his
intentions.   When compelled to retire, these advanced
squadrons should concentrate in échelon positions; and
ultimately either pass through intervals in their own
line or round its flanks, and range themselves in reserve
prepared for whatever duty may be required of them.

132. The formation of a fleet in two parallel lines
in chequered order (fig. 19), the ships in the second

Fig. 19.

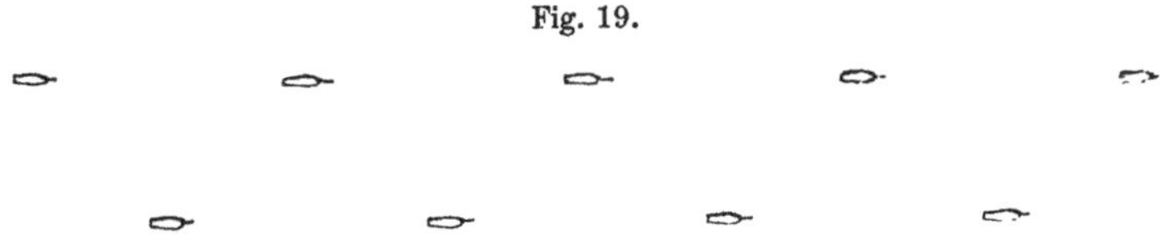

line covering the intervals between those in the first
line, is a convenient order of steaming, though by no
means a good order of battle; since, to enable the
ships in the second line to defend the intervals in the
first, or to enable them to form the two lines into one,

the intervals between all the ships in each line, as well as between the two lines, must be very great—at least equal to two cables' length. It would be better that the ships in the front line should be ranged at the usual distance of one cable's length, and that the second line should constitute a reserve force ready to move in any direction that might be required.

133. With a fleet of sailing ships the operation of doubling upon an enemy's line can only be made upon the rear ships of a fleet under sail to leeward, by slanting towards them, supposing these to be sailing *on the wind* on the same tack. In all such operations there is great difficulty in keeping sailing ships, on either side, in proper positions,—one on the bow, and the opposite one on the quarter of the ship attacked,—so that the attacking ships may not fire into each other.

134. The most skilful, brilliant, and successful battle fought by Nelson, and perhaps ever fought on the sea, was assuredly that in which he attacked the French fleet at anchor in Aboukir Bay, in 1798, by doubling upon the French van in such a manner that seven French ships were attacked on both sides by eleven British ships, whilst the rear of the French fleet anchored head to wind, and therefore to leeward, could render the van no succour.

The French fleet consisting of thirteen sail of the line was anchored in line ahead N.W., the van ship about 2400 yards distant from a shoal, between which and the van it was never imagined that the British fleet could pass.[a] The intervals between the ships of the French line were 160 yards, and the length of the line, including the length of the ships, was about one and a half mile.

The French admiral concluding that Nelson would postpone his attack till the morrow, as the day was far

---

[a] Lord Nelson, observing that the French ships were at single anchor, had the sagacity to perceive that the French admiral must have ascertained that the depth of water between the van ship and the shoal was sufficient to allow that ship to swing round on her anchor in the event of a change of the wind ; and on this assumption the plan of attack was determined.

advanced, remained at anchor for the night, laying out his anchors in such a manner as to spring the broadsides of his ships towards his opponent. But he was deceived. Nelson formed his fourteen ships into two divisions, one of which was to pass athwart the van of the French fleet, between it and the shoal, and attack the ships on the interior side, whilst the ships of the other division were to range themselves on the exterior side, so that every French ship, down to the seventh, the 'Orient,' should be attacked by two British ships, one on the port bow or stern, the other on the starboard quarter or bow. For this each British ship prepared to anchor by the stern, passing a stream cable out of her gun-room-port and tricing it up alongside, beneath the lower deck ports, bending it to the bow anchor on that side; so that by paying out the cable when the anchor was let go, the ship might be brought up by the stern, and thus having two cables attached to the same anchor, the ship's broadside might be "sprung" into the proper direction for action, by slackening one cable and hauling upon the other. Thus eleven British ships doubled upon the seven van ships of the French fleet with the utmost skill and regularity; and in that celebrated action which began about 5 P.M., while the British ships did no injury to one another they captured all those to which they were opposed. The French admiral committed a great mistake in not getting under way as soon as the British fleet appeared.

135. A steam fleet will never be caught in so helpless a position; the ships would have their steam up, get under way, and try the issue of a general action; or the ships not doubled upon in this mode of attack might rush up and double upon one or both of the attacking divisions.

The tactical skill evinced by Nelson in this great battle was a practical exemplification of that maxim in military tactics, which teaches the importance of so conducting a battle as to bring upon the point of attack a great superiority of force, in such manner that

the enemy, even if numerically superior upon the
whole, might be unable to succour the part so over-
powered—a maxim to the application of which Napoleon I. owed mainly his triumphs, and which Nelson
so skilfully adopted in the battle of the Nile.   Had the
French fleet been anchored in two lines, Nelson either
would not have attempted this audacious mode of attack ;
or if he had, one or other of his divisions must have
been placed between two divisions of his enemy—an
observation which the author here makes to show the
evils of extending a fleet, whether at anchor or under
sail, in a single line, and the importance of always
ranging fleets in two lines, or, at least, with a strong
reserve in a second line.

Doubling upon the ships of an enemy's fleet, will,
however, be hereafter an important evolution in the
offensive movements of steam fleets ; but this must be
managed very differently from that which has heretofore been practised, and should rather be by doubling
upon the van and throwing it into confusion, than by
attacking the rear of a fleet.

136. It would be a hazardous undertaking to endeavour to penetrate the line of a steam fleet ranged in
order of battle en échelon, as in fig. 16, p. 100, the
ships of the attacking fleet moving in directions contrary to those of the fleet attacked, for all the lines
of fire from the ships in that order are open in every
direction ; and those from two ships at least would
cross each other upon any one ship which might
be advancing to penetrate the line of battle.   A ship
in the act of penetrating, and after having penetrated,
would assuredly be in a thoroughly crippled state.   It
is obvious, however, that the intervals between ships
en échelon, on any line of bearing, are open in all their
width to the ships of an enemy's fleet coming up on
the same course as is kept by the ships in that line, for
the purpose of cutting through it : but a fleet so coming
up, suppose in line ahead, towards the interval between
the ships B and C, fig. 16, and parallel to the directions
of those ships, would find itself opposed in its advance

by fires from the starboard broadsides of the ships A
and B; and, should they succeed in passing the interval,
by fires from the port broadsides of the ships C and D:
at the same time they would be liable to a general
enfilade, first from the stern-guns, and then from the
bow-guns of such of the ships as are nearly in the
directions of their courses.   Supposing the penetration
to be effected, the ships on either side of the line of
penetration might, with ease, move up and immediately
put the ships which had got through between two fires.

137. In an attack from the windward by a fleet of
sailing ships, it was necessary that these should bear
down directly or obliquely on the broadside batteries of
the enemy's ships, though in so doing they were unavoidably exposed to a severe fire, more or less raking,
before they could attain a position favourable for close
action or for penetrating his line.   Sailing ships have
invariably been severely crippled in sails and rigging
as well as in the hulls, in bearing down upon ships to
leeward, even when gunnery fire was far less efficient
than it is now.   The ships of Lord Duncan's fleet, in
bearing down upon the Dutch line, were far more severely
damaged in the hull than in any actions against the
French; and so assuredly would Nelson's division have
been treated in bearing down in line ahead at Trafalgar,
if the French and Spanish gunnery had been then-as
efficient as that of the Dutch fleet proved at Camperdown, and as that of the French navy is at the present
time.

138. An examination of the tactical circumstances of
the battle of Trafalgar will show that Villeneuve's plan
was to abandon the vicious practice of extending a fleet,
in line ahead, in a single line of battle; he apparently
intended to contract, concentrate, and range his force
in such manner as to render the penetration of his line
from the windward extremely difficult, and to give his
fleet military strength by the reciprocal defence of its
ships.   Villeneuve's nautical science was in advance of
the practical methods of that day; and it did present
great obstacles to the success of Nelson's plan of attack,

which would not have been experienced if each French
and Spanish ship had been in the wake of the ship
before it, in single line of battle.   There can be no
doubt that the novel formation which Villeneuve attempted, though frustrated by the disabilities of the
sail, shadows forth the adoption of that order of battle
which the author has endeavoured to propound, and
which will undoubtedly hereafter become an established
formation in steam warfare.

The combined French and Spanish fleets previous
to the action off Trafalgar, when seen a little before
daybreak on the 21st of October, were in line ahead on
the starboard tack, extending over a space of nearly five
miles.   At 8 h. 30 m. A.M. the ships tacked together by
signal, and formed on the port tack, very irregularly, as
it seemed, in a crescent figure, convex to leeward (James,
vol. iv. p. 32).   Lord Collingwood in his official despatch stated, that in this novel formation every
ship (as a, b, c, &c., a', b', c', &c.), fig. 20, was about

Fig. 20.

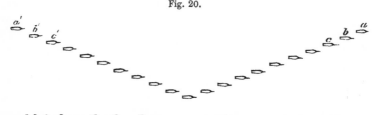

a cable's length ahead or astern of its respective following or leading ship.   Thus the combined fleet seemed
to be formed in a kind of double line, which, when
viewed on the beam, appeared to leave very small
intervals between the ships.

This formation, which to some appeared disorderly,
to the experienced eye of Admiral Collingwood gave
indications of a wisely-considered plan, designed for
the purpose of making the fleets occupy a less extent
of space, and thus enabling the ships to concentrate and
combine their strength by reciprocal fire.   It failed, as
we have said, from circumstances over which the commander of the combined fleet could have no control;

but great is the credit due to the illustrious commander of the British fleet for having thus, in the apparent disorder, discovered a new principle in naval tactics— one which would present very great obstacles to an attempt of the enemy to penetrate a line of ships.

It is now evident that Admiral Villeneuve's intention was to form the combined fleet in two lines of bearing, with the angular point to leeward ; thus reversing the order of retreat described in Art. 114. This formation, though difficult to be effected, and scarcely possible to be long retained, by sailing ships, is capable of easy accomplishment and retention with a fleet of steamers. The dispositions of the several ships may be understood from the above figure and description.

139. It is extremely probable that, if the present improved state of naval gunnery had existed, in 1805, in the French navy, the divisions of the British fleet, in bearing down upon the combined French and Spanish fleet off Trafalgar, would have been entirely disabled before they came to close action.   Nelson's and Collingwood's divisions advanced at a rate not exceeding $1\frac{1}{2}$ miles per hour, and the ' Victory ' was under the fire of some hundreds of heavy guns during forty minutes before she reached the enemy's line.   According to M. de la Gravière (*Guerres Maritimes*, vol. ii., pp. 185 to 188, Plunkett's translation), Nelson would have seen his ships smashed to pieces by those of the French, like cavalry when improperly attempting to break the squares of steady infantry.   " This disregard of established rules in approaching an enemy arose entirely," writes M. de la Gravière, in a note referring to the French translation of the author's work on Naval Gunnery, " out of particular circumstances, and may be considered as a proof of the decline in French gunnery-practice during the war."

140. But in the tactics of fleets endowed with adequate steam-power, there need be no such exposure to damage, before a position for close action can be attained.   A steam fleet so endowed, instead of bearing

down obliquely or directly, on the broadside batteries of
an enemy's fleet, may run up from the rear, in two
divisions, alongside of the enemy's ships, in an order
parallel to his line, and thus double upon it with safety.
This could be prevented only by the enemy being
protected by a strong reserve en échelon, covering his
rear.   Between this reserve and the main line, and
exposed to the fire of both, the attacking division would
be obliged to pass, in order to effect its object.

141. Success in this mode of attack depends upon
the comparative speed of the two fleets.   If the fleet of
the assailant be superior to that of the enemy, the latter
cannot avoid close action on disadvantageous terms.
If, on the contrary, the speed of the fleet menaced is
superior to that of the other, that fleet will be able to
make its escape.

It may appear to some readers, that if, as stated in
Art. 139, in future naval battles, there will be no attacks
by fleets advancing directly in divisions of ships arrayed
in line ahead on the broadside batteries of an enemy's
fleet, as at Trafalgar, and that there will be no repeti-
tion of such a battle as that in Aboukir Bay—Nelson's
two crowning victories,—this would tend to show that
the new system of naval warfare will put an end to that
bold, resolute, and audacious mode of action, which was
the wont of the British navy.   But this will not be the
case.   It is true that, in the present very improved
state of naval gunnery, such a mode of attack as that
adopted at Trafalgar could not be made without seriously crippling the attacking fleet, before it could close
with the enemy ; and it is not probable that so faulty a
formation as that of the French fleet in Aboukir Bay
will again occur.   But, our officers, imbued with the
resources of tactical science and nautical skill, and our
men able and ardent to carry out, with unflinching
courage, their commands, will nevertheless find in steam
warfare, ample opportunities for acting in that vigorous
and audacious manner which has ever been congenial
to the spirit of British seamen.

142. The operation of doubling upon the rear of a

fleet of sailing ships, ranged in a single line ahead, as
A B, fig. 21, was obviously invited by the inherent

Fig. 21.

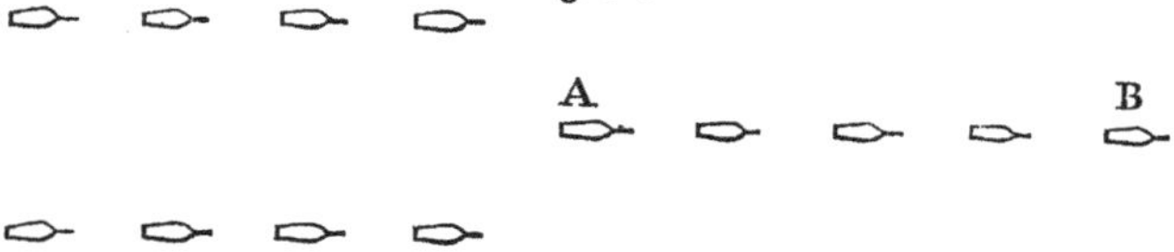

weakness of such an order of battle; and, employed
against such a line, it was in truth a very formidable
mode of attack : but fleets of steam-ships ranged in line,
as A B, fig. 22, with a good reserve, as C D, would, if

Fig. 22.

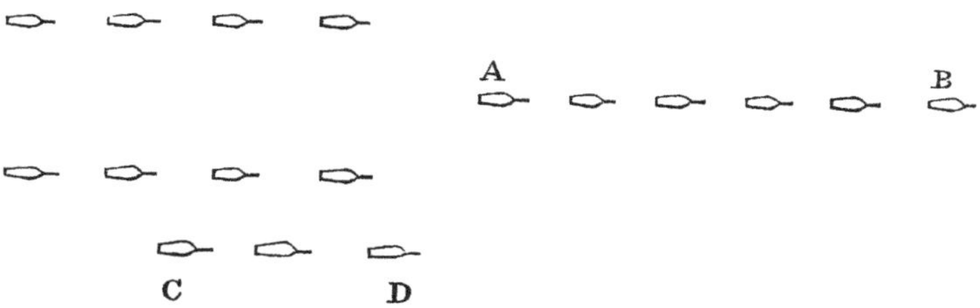

commanded by experienced tacticians, have little to
apprehend in such a case. It might be met by the
reciprocal operation of doubling, by means of the reserve, upon that division of the enemy that might
endeavour to penetrate between the rear of the fleet
and the reserve, by which that rear is covered and
protected.

A well-commanded steam-fleet should not passively
receive, in its existing order, an attack made upon it,
but should rather assume promptly a position in which
it may, by offensive operations, actively resist and frustrate the enemy's attempt. Thus (fig. 23, p. 116) if,
being already in line ahead, as at A B, the ships in the
positions a, a, &c., with a reserve as C D, and the ships
in positions c, c, &c., the enemy advancing in two lines
E F, G H, should make demonstrations for attacking at
the rear, or doubling the fleet; the ships in A B may

immediately be thrown en échelon in the positions e, e, &c., while those in the reserve may take the positions d, d,

Fig. 23.

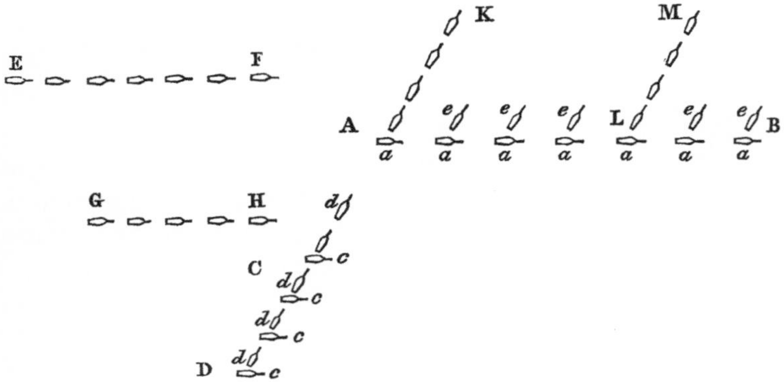

&c.   The enemy then, instead of finding the rear of the fleet unprotected, will find himself exposed in both his advancing lines, to a direct fire from the broadside batteries of the ships in line and in reserve, as they cross his bows, while the sterns of all are refused to him. The rear half of the line A B may now form itself on the line A K, and the other half on L M, parallel to it and supporting it ; in this order of battle the fleet might engage the enemy at the head of his lines and compel him to fight on very disadvantageous terms.   The enemy's attempt, therefore, would in all probability terminate in his discomfiture; of which, in course, advantage would be immediately taken.   Counter manœuvres may be promptly made by steam fleets to meet, and, if well conducted, to frustrate, almost any manœuvres that may be attempted.

143. A well-exercised and skilfully-commanded steam-fleet should never be restricted to pure passive defence. Steam propulsion is essentially an active agent which seeks the initiative, and invigorates execution ; it should therefore always be employed promptly and vigorously in offensive operations.   A celebrated tactician has

well said that it is in offensive operations, and not in
passive resistance, that decisive victories are to be
found.[a]

144. The advance of a fleet of sailing ships in line
abreast, is an extremely difficult and disadvantageous
movement, as the ships are exposed to be raked fore and
aft, and this order itself it is extremely difficult to maintain with the sail. (See Art. 89, Note, p. 79.)   But a
fleet ranged en échelon is in a very favourable order
for approaching an enemy obliquely, the ships not being
exposed, in their advance, to an enfilading or raking
fire.   A steam-fleet may advance in line abreast with
as much precision as an army on land can march in
line of columns ; and, when near the enemy, the ships,
by being thrown into échelon order, may avoid being
raked or enfiladed.   It should be observed that a ship
cannot, strictly speaking, be raked unless she is so near
the enemy that the trajectory, or path of the shot, is
nearly horizontal : if the distance of the ships is great
enough to require the shot to be fired at an elevation
which will cause the path to have considerable curvature in the vertical direction, the ship may be fired
into, but not raked.

145. When a line of troops, advancing in close
columns, comes so near the enemy's position that batteries placed on the alignments of these solid masses
would become destructive, the deep order of the column
is extended into a slender line of troops ; so, ships
advancing in line abreast, when arrived so near the
enemy as to be exposed to a raking or enfilading fire,
may form themselves into a line en échelon, in which
order they may advance obliquely under cover of a
cross fire from their bow and broadside guns ; and,
when close to the enemy, may form in line ahead if
they can do no better.

146. The great tactical maxim taught by modern
military science is to abandon the practice of fighting
in parallel order, and so to combine offensive move-

---

[a] " C'est dans une action offensive, et non dans la résistance, qu'est la vic-
toire."— LLOYD.

ments as to bring a superior force to bear upon some
decisive point of attack,[a] thus rendering the attacking
troops stronger upon that point than the enemy, whatever be his entire numerical strength.   By the oblique
order of attack this important maxim may be applied
in the tactics of steam-fleets, with as much certainty as
in military operations on land.

147. The oblique order in a steam-fleet may be formed
by ships in line ahead, or by ships in échelon upon a line
of bearing parallel to that of the enemy, the obliquity
of the ships to their line of bearing constituting in
reality an oblique order.   The degree of obliquity of
these formations, in military tactics, depends chiefly on
the nature of the ground; but in naval operations on
the uniform surface of the sea, the military maxim,
that the degree of obliquity should in general be half a
right angle (" à demi-quart de conversion " — *Guibert*),
should be absolute.

148. In an oblique order of battle, advancing to
attack an enemy in line, the ships must of necessity be
ranged in line ahead; for, if in échelon upon a line of
bearing oblique to the enemy's line, the ships so ranged
would be steaming directly towards the enemy, exposed
to be enfiladed quite as much as if they were advancing
in line abreast.

149. Oblique orders of battle, when speaking of two
opposing fleets, each in line ahead, are of two kinds :
1st, when the fleets are steaming towards each other
as if their courses would meet in some point, as P
(fig. 24), in lines making with each other an acute angle ;
and 2ndly, when the fleets are standing towards each
other as if their courses would meet in some point, as Q
(fig. 25), in lines making with each other an obtuse angle.
In technical language the latter is called the cross attack,
and both these movements are preparatory to attacks on

---

[a] " Le *principe* fondamental de toutes les combinaisons militaires, consiste
à opérer avec la plus grande masse de ses forces, un effort combiné sur le point
décisif.   Le premier *moyen* est, de prendre l'initiative des mouvements, car il
est incontestable, qu'une armée, en prenant l'initiative d'un mouvement, peut
le cacher jusqu'à l'instant où il est en pleine exécution."—Jomini, tom. iii.
p. 345.

the van of an enemy's line. In both cases it is clear that
whichever fleet can, by superior speed, so forereach upon

Fig. 24.

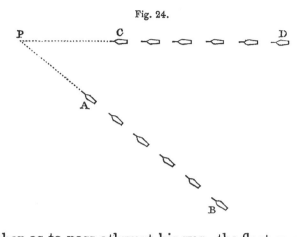

the other as to pass athwart his van, the fleet so gained
upon will be placed at manifest disadvantage; the van-
ships will first receive obliquely the broadside fire of

Fig. 25.

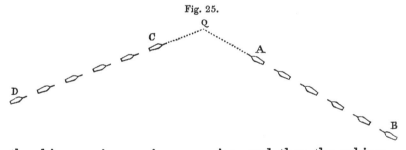

the ships coming up in succession, and then the raking
fire of those that are passing athwart their bows. Those
van-ships, being in no condition to attempt the hazardous movement of passing on through the enemy's line,
by which they have been outflanked, would be compelled
to break off from their course, and, in confusion, would
endeavour to assume some other formation.

A steam-fleet should avoid battle in an order parallel
to the enemy's line, steaming on a contrary course;
since the movement leads only to a cannonade, with,

perhaps, equal injury to both fleets, and ends generally
in a drawn battle, of which there are many instances,
to the mortification of the commanders and the disap-
pointment of the country.   Such was Keppel's action
in 1788, and such would have been the case in the
battle of the 12th April, 1782 (in which the French
and English fleets were passing each other on contrary
tacks), had not Rodney, perceiving that the enemy's
line was not kept compact, seized the favourable
opportunity, and severed the French line of battle by
penetrating its centre.   (See Art. 87.)

150. It must be observed that ships in single line
ahead, though in one sense in a line of battle, form
nevertheless a long and slender column, which, when outflanked, is in the same predicament as a line of troops
in the field, in like manner outflanked and turned.[a]
The fleet and the army would be equally thrown into
confusion.

151. In the case of the cross attack, that fleet which
crosses athwart the other has manifestly the advantage.   In sailing-tactics, the object so much contended
for was to *fetch* to windward of the enemy's van or rear.
In the tactics of steam-fleets, it is clear that the advantage of forereaching upon and attacking the enemy in
van or rear, is entirely a question of steam-speed; and
the importance of a superiority in this respect is therefore manifest.[b]

152. In the battle of the 14th February, 1797, when
the squadron of the Spanish fleet, which had formed to
leeward, failed in its attempt to reunite with the body
of the fleet by passing through the British line, the
fleets tacked to the N.W.   In this course it was pur-
sued by the British van, led by the ' Culloden,' and
followed by the ' Blenheim,' ' Prince George,' and others,
whose superior speed enabled them ultimately to forereach upon and attack the Spanish van, where the

---

[a] " Une colonne profonde attaquée par la tête est dans la même situation
qu'une ligne attaquée à son extremité."—JOMINI, tom. iii. p. 347.
[b] See Art. 95, Note.

principal prizes, viz., the 'Santissima Trinidada,' the 'San Nicholas,' and the 'San Josef,' were taken.

153. A fleet in line or lines ahead, is far more likely to be thrown into disorder by being thus attacked at the head, than by any attempt on the rear. An attack on the rear may be frustrated (as in fig. 23, p. 116) by having there a reserve of ships, overlapping and covering that extremity of the line; and the rear of a fleet, like the rear of a column of troops, may be disordered without throwing the whole fleet into confusion. On the contrary, when a column is disordered by being attacked at head, that disorder recoils upon the whole column. The rear of a fleet may be attacked by an enemy in parallel order, but the van of a fleet can only be attacked by a fleet moving towards it in oblique order. (See Art. 149.)

154. The great advantage of échelon formations consists in the facility which is afforded to the commander of a fleet for embarrassing the enemy by demonstrations which he may think fit to make in order to mask his real intentions. False demonstrations may promptly be executed with a view of deceiving the enemy respecting an intended point of attack. Misled by the position assumed by the ships, the enemy may be tempted to change his dispositions; on discovering his error he will make an effort to rectify it, perhaps under fire, and in the midst of the confusion attending the change of disposition, a vigorous attack being made upon him will, in all probability, end in his total defeat.

155. Let an enemy's fleet be moving in any direction in line ahead, as A B (fig. 26, p. 122), and let a fleet be advancing en échelon, as C D, the ships being disposed as shown at *a b* preparatory to an attack on the enemy at the head (B) of his line. This disposition of the ships can be promptly changed to *c d*, at right angles to *a b*, as if for the purpose of attacking the rear (A) of the line, by turning each ship through a quarter of a circle; while a fleet in line ahead, in the position A B, would be obliged to reverse the courses of all the

I

ships. Thus either extremity, whether van or rear, of
a fleet may be menaced, and the reverse extremity

Fig. 26.

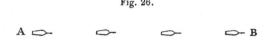

actually assailed with great facility, while the commander of the fleet is kept to the last moment in a
state of uncertainty respecting the real point of attack.

The enemy in the position A B may, no doubt, change
his order from line ahead into line en échelon : in
that case the order of his advance should be such that
the fleets may, cæteris paribus, be on equal terms. Either
fleet may be forced to turn into line ahead, and by a
speedy movement menace the flank of the other.   When
en échelon, it must be remarked, however, that, in the
conflicts of well-commanded steam-fleets, feigned attacks
may produce serious realities to the fleet making the
feint, if the position of the enemy should be such as to
permit him to penetrate with a division, in force, between the body of the fleet and the attacking division.
Therefore, unless the enemy's fleet be extended in
line, and the main body of the attacking fleet be in a
position to support the feint with great force, any
attempt to engage in that manner would be attended
with considerable danger.

156. A vigorous initiative, promptly taken, as soon
as the force of an enemy's fleet and its order of steaming can be distinctly ascertained, afterwards prosecuted
without faltering by a tactician having a clear perception of what he has to do, and of the way in which
it should be done, will force an enemy to range his
ships in the order in which he means to fight, or to
manœuvre in order to avoid or postpone an action.   If

the enemy would simply manœuvre, a trial of skill will ensue between the admirals of the two fleets; and he who is best exercised in tactical evolutions, and can conduct them with the greatest skill, will out-manœuvre the other, and bring him to action in the circumstances most advantageous for himself.

If, on the contrary, the enemy determine to fight, he will be forced, by a resolute advance of the fleet, to extend his line in order of battle, as at A B, fig. 8, p. 92. Whatever that order may be, he should be immediately attacked while so extended. An oblique movement of the fleet, supposed to be in double columns, as at l, n, p, should be made towards the right, on the enemy's rear, and a demonstration to menace seriously that part of his line. This may be effected by the whole fleet steaming in the order represented at m, n, p, in fig. 8, and, at the same time, the steam frigates and sloops moving to the right, supported by the reserve, should advance as if to attack, and double upon the rear B, of the enemy's line. This menace should be put in execution before any change in the order of the fleet's advance has been made, which might indicate the real intention; but, when the demonstration shall have led the enemy to draw his reserve ships to the support of his rear, the divisions l, n, p, of the attacking fleet, previously formed in échelon of lines on their respective centre ships, should rush up successively, in that order, at full speed, to the left. When close to the enemy they should engage, and, if possible, outflank his van, while the right division p, supported by the reserve (which will be withdrawn as soon as the feint has produced the intended effect and the real attack has commenced), will vigorously attack and charge through his centre with a superiority of force, and either penetrate it or create a mêlée which shall render it impossible for the rear ships to rejoin their leaders; at the same time the commander of the enemy's fleet will be quite unable to reverse the courses of his van ships, in order to double upon the division attacking his centre.

No doubt some of the ships will, in these attacks, be
seriously injured, but it may be reasonably expected
that none will be so entirely disabled in their screws,
or otherwise, as to be prevented from arresting the progress of the enemy's rear ships. Some of those, at
least, which had attacked and penetrated the centre,
may, after having effected this object, turn into line
ahead to the left, and attack on the starboard side that
part of the enemy's fleet which had been previously
attacked on the port side.

Should an attack thus conducted have a successful
issue, half the ships constituting the enemy's line might
be captured or destroyed, and then all the available
ships of the fleet, with the reserve steam frigates and
sloops, should be sent in pursuit of the retiring enemy.
Such may not be the result of a battle under the conditions assumed in this article ; the author professes
only to have described a vigorous mode of action consistent with the tactical principles which arise from
the employment of the new motive power in naval
warfare.

157. The operation of reversing steam-ships (300
or 350 feet in length) when in line of battle, and under
the guns of an enemy, is a difficult and dangerous evolution, which should be avoided if possible ; and in well-
planned battles the operation should scarcely be necessary. It may be inferred, however, from what has
been stated in Art. 91, that the operation of reversing
the ships of a fleet may be occasionally useful, and even
necessary : for example, the van of a fleet being cut off
from its rear, in consequence of the line being penetrated at its centre by an enemy's fleet, is thrown out of
action, and can in no other way succour the rear than
by reversing simultaneously the ships, and doubling,
in its turn, upon that division of the enemy's fleet which,
after the penetration, had enveloped its rear.

158. Steam ships in line may easily reverse their
courses individually ; but to reverse the alignment of a
fleet by changing the flanks, moving the ships in the
looped curves which they must respectively describe in

order to maintain in the new line the same order that they had in the original formation, is an evolution wholly useless and utterly impracticable on real service. It is like the obsolete military movement of changing the front and flanks of a division of troops to the rear. The alignment of a fleet of twenty ships covers a space of at least two miles. The ship A on the right flank would have to describe a curve of more than that length to gain the right A of the reversed line, whilst the ship on the left B would have to describe looped curves of still greater extent in order to get into her position B' on the left flank ; and all the intermediate ships would have to describe very complex curves in order to attain their respective stations in the new alignment. The nature of these movements may be understood from the annexed figure (fig. 27). The

Fig. 27.

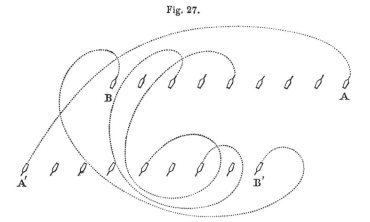

necessity of putting ships to the right-about can scarcely be required under any circumstances, unless, indeed, it be to turn their sterns to the enemy and make off, which should never be done. But, should it become necessary to reverse the position of a line of ships already in line abreast, so as to arrange them again in line abreast, but facing in opposite directions, the ships should be reversed individually. This may be done by two movements : first, the ships should be put in line ahead by a quarter-turn of each ship to starboard or port, and then into the required position by another quarter-turn of each in the same direction. The new line will be in rear of the former, and in inverted order, the right wing being now the left, and *vice versâ* ; in military parlance *clubbed*: this position is not now considered objectionable in military evolutions, when sudden changes of front to the rear are required.

159. The modes of attack above noticed have not been introduced with any expectation that they will be considered as model operations, or that they will apply as precise rules for conducting naval battles. No such rules can be prescribed ; and the author has stated these cases merely to develope principles of action. The accidents of a sea-fight are so various, the manner of conducting the evolutions, though simplified by steam, yet so complex, that only a few general principles can be laid down by science ; the rest must be left to the skill, the genius, and the mental resources of a chief in applying the principles to each particular case as it arises.

160. There can be no doubt that in the conflicts of fleets, conducted with energy and resolution, with all the capabilities of steam propulsion, there will be occasional mêlées, of ships getting confusedly in contiguity with one another, which may by chance or design lead to a boarding. This last will introduce a class of operations of a military character, for which we ought to be well prepared. A line-of-battle ship once alongside of an enemy must either assault or be assaulted : steam-ships should therefore be provided with larger quotas of troops, habituated to the sea, than heretofore, and should be provided with some better facilities for boarding an enemy than scrambling along yards or booms with their cutlasses between their teeth ; and there should be some deck defences by which to repulse a sudden rush of the enemy when he has obtained a footing.

161. The assault of a military work is facilitated by ladders or other means of getting into it : means should therefore be provided to gain the deck of an

enemy's ship by a temporary bridging; and every ship should be provided with means of resisting an assault when actually boarded. All military works, from a regular fortress to a field redoubt, are invariably furnished with some description of interior defence, by which the temporary success of an assault may not be followed by the entire subjugation of the work. Loopholed barricades should be placed across the terminations of the quarter-decks and forecastles, and other defensive arrangements should be made to repel boarders. And there might be vertical scuttles, where horizontal scuttles were of old, between the guns, on the fighting decks of ships, to serve as loopholes for Minié marksmen there placed. The fire of the Minié rifle at Sebastopol was so deadly as to pick off the loaders, spongers, and others of the guns' crews through the embrasures of the parapets; and to save the men as much as possible it was necessary to provide shot-proof mantlets, which were placed across the internal openings of the embrasures. Expert riflemen, firing through scuttles made as formerly on the fighting decks of ships, might pick off the spongers, loaders, and tacklemen of a gun, through the large gun-ports which ships armed with the heavy guns of the present day require, in order to be enabled to give a sufficiently elevated, depressed, or oblique fire from the ship. (The ordinary size of a gun-port is about 3 feet square; the ports of the 'Diadem' and vessels of her class similarly armed are 4 feet 6 inches wide, and 3 feet 10 inches high.) Skilful riflemen firing at an aperture of that size, at from 400 to 800 yards distance, would unquestionably soon put a gun's crew hors-de-combat. No mantlets can be used to cover the loaders, and, therefore, some other expedient is required to protect them from so destructive a fire.[a]

162. That assaults by boarding will hereafter be frequent and formidable in naval warfare, is an opinion

---

[a] The author is prepared with a means to effect this, but which for the present he reserves.

very prevalent among French officers ; Admiral De la
Susse in his answer to Question 260, proposed to him by
L'Enquête Parlementaire, vol. ii. p. 84, says he attaches
the greatest importance to the project of providing ships
which may be capable of assaulting the enemy at close
quarters with strong garrisons of troops ; as well as of
rendering ships more capable of resisting assaults ; and
Admiral de la Gravière writes :—" Les abordages pré-
médités sont devenus très rares aujourd'hui, parceque
c'est une manœuvre toujours dangereuse à tenter.   Avec
les navires à vapeur ils seront beaucoup plus fré-
quents.   Une fois les navires ainsi accrochés, on pouvait
s'élancer sur le pont ennemi, le sabre aux dents et le
pistolet au poing, ce serait une mêlée, une affaire d'arme
blanche, dans laquelle l'élan et le courage auraient beau
jeu ; mais les deux navires, bien qu'accrochés, sont encore
séparés par un intervalle de dix ou douze pieds : si
quelque mât sert à les réunir, c'est un pont qui offre à
peine passage à deux hommes de front."—*Guerres Maritimes*, tom. ii. pp. 259, 260.

163. It is especially in the power of reaping more
abundantly the fruits of victory that the active agency
of steam will be felt.   Many great victories have been
won without being followed up to their ultimate results,
because the sails and rigging of the victorious ships have
been so much damaged that they could not pursue the
flying enemy.   It will not be so with steam fleets, particularly with fleets of screw-steamers : their masts may
be shot away, but the submerged machine by which they
are moved, if kept free from entanglement, is inaccessible
to shot; and if the commander of a victorious fleet use it
not, in vigorously following up any advantage which he
may have gained, he would justly be censured ; and the
country would not be satisfied if a barren victory only
were gained.

164. It has been shown in the course of this work
that the order of battle in line ahead for a fleet consisting of a single column of ships, though most convenient for simple broadside action when the opposing
fleets are within gunshot of one another, is yet one of

considerable weakness. (See Arts. 84, 106, 125, 150.) By a fleet of steamers it may be attacked and doubled upon in the van or rear, or it may be cut somewhere in its length by a fleet moving across its line of direction, and thus, a portion, severed from the rest of the fleet, may be captured or destroyed. In fact, the order in line ahead is particularly exposed to an attack made in conformity to the general principle in war — " the greatest force possible should be brought to act against a weak part of the line attacked." The mode of strengthening it has been stated ; and it is shown that, by means of a strong reserve squadron, the effort of the enemy may be paralyzed, and may even be made to revert against himself (Art. 142). It is shown (Art. 107) that the order in line abreast for steamers may, with advantage, be assumed when the fleet is not very close to the enemy's line, on account of the facility with which the ships may be turned from this position to any other that may be required.

The author has dwelt much on the disposition of ships in lines of bearing, or in what may be called the échelon formation ; and his object has been to show the advantages which this formation has over others in respect of the reciprocal defence which the ships are able to afford each other (Art. 128), and in respect of the facility which that disposition, like the line abreast, affords for changing the position of the ships in their line of bearing, as well as for changing the position of the line itself (Art. 169) : by this facility, an order of battle on the offensive may be, almost immediately, converted into an order for defence, and *vice versâ*. The échelon formation lends itself particularly to that order of battle with steamers in which the ships are formed upon two lines of bearing, for advance or retreat, making with each other an angle which may generally be of 90°, though occasionally of more (Arts. 114, 118, 156).

165. A fleet divided into two or more double columns of this kind is in a highly advantageous order to advance against an enemy in line ahead : the divisions

are thus capable of being directed to a part of the line
which may be discovered to be weaker than the rest,
whether that part be the van, the rear, or the centre of
the line; and the movements may be regulated so as to
leave the commander of the enemy's fleet in doubt on
what part of his line the shock may take place (Art.
154). If thought fit, the divisions may, with no difficulty, be formed into line ahead, parallel to that of the
enemy, or into divisions en échelon oblique to that of
the enemy, and in this order may cut or turn his line
of battle.

The disposition of ships in line en échelon affords a
more complete system of reciprocal defence among the
ships than can be obtained by any other arrangement;
the fires from guns in the bow or stern batteries of the
ships cross with those from the broadside batteries over
the spaces between the ships, and also to the extent of
some hundred yards ahead or astern of the general line
(Art. 128).

This principle of reciprocal and flanking defence
may be carried out, with steam-fleets, so far as to com-
prehend the disposition in line of battle, strengthened
by placing ships on wings obliquely to the general line;
and, in the case of a very long line, forming some
ships on a double line of bearing in front of the line
itself (Art. 130).

It is hoped that the principles inculcated in this
work will be found sufficiently intelligible to enable a
good tactician to apply them in any form of battle
which he may initiate, or which he may assume, either
for the purpose of counteracting any measures taken
by the enemy, or to take advantage of any false movement which he may make.

166. In order to bring sailing ships into positions
which may enable them to attack land batteries and
maritime fortresses with the advantage which proxi-
mity gives to a fleet or squadron in such a case, steam-
tugs may, and have been used. The Prince de Join-
ville's attack of Tangiers in 1844 is a proof of what
steam may effect by traction; but, if well opposed, this

mode of approach would perhaps be both dangerous and uncertain, from the difficulty of passing a tow-rope, and the probability of its breaking or being cut by a shot, besides the risk of the steam-tug being disabled, as was the case with the Danish ship, the ' Christian the Eighth.' (See Colonel Stevens' account of that catastrophe.)

In the naval attack of Sevastopol in 1854, each sail-ing ship was led to its station by a steam-tug lashed alongside, and this is a more effectual method of gain-ing the end than that of towing would be ; but the best application of steam-power for battle purposes is evi-dently that in which the propulsion is inherent in the ship itself.

During the war with Russia in 1852-4 the Govern-ment of this country, impressed with the importance of having a numerous flotilla of steamers, of dimensions which would permit them to manœuvre in shallow waters, caused a considerable number of such vessels to be constructed ; and these being capable of pene-trating into creeks, or moving along a shore to which large vessels could not approach, it was intended that they should be extensively employed in the Baltic and the Black Seas.   One kind of these vessels, which were called *Despatch Gun-Boats*, are from 180 to 200 feet in length, and from $28\frac{1}{3}$ to 30 feet in breadth ; their draught of water is 11 feet 4 inches, and their burthen 450 tons : they are propelled by screws, and their horse-power is 160.   Their great length, in proportion to their breadth, is a serious cause of weakness in these vessels, as it is very difficult to tye them well together *in midships*, and they are very liable to twisting strains in heavy seas.   The guns are mounted on pivot-car-riages and slides, in the body of the ship ; the one abaft, and the other before the funnel.   In voyaging the guns are housed longitudinally in the middle of the deck.

A smaller class of steam vessels has since been con-structed as gun-boats, and these come fully up to the author's idea of what a good gun-boat should be.   Their dimensions are—in length 100 feet, extreme breadth 22 feet, depth of hold 7 feet 10 inches; and draught of water at the load-line 6 feet 6 inches; their burthen is 212 tons; they have two engines, each of 30 horse-power, and they are armed with a 68-pounder of 95 cwt. These vessels are lugger-rigged without bowsprit, and they are sufficiently strong to bear that heavy gun at either, or at both ends, for action.

167. The means of reducing to practice the principles which are to operate the vast change in naval tactics caused by the use of steam as a moving power in ships of war may, to many persons, appear to involve very serious difficulties; and, perhaps, to some, those diffi-culties may seem insurmountable. Such, indeed, they would be if it were attempted, without previous expe-rience, to execute the more complex formations, which are occasionally required. Officers and men should, however, be made familiar with such formations with steam-fleets, beginning with those of the most elementary nature, as the disposition of ships in simple lines of bearing, and proceeding to the formations of columns in double lines of bearing : they should also be exercised in the practice of the evolutions required in the various circumstances of attack and defence.

Much study will be required on the part of naval officers to enable them to understand thoroughly the principles and objects of naval warfare with steam; and, with this, much must still be left to individual judgment when an officer would put those principles in practice, or direct those who are to execute the opera-tions under his superintendence.

The disposition of a fleet in divisions, consisting of double columns en échelon, in lines of bearing, as shown in fig. 8, p. 92, may be considered as the general order of steaming in which a fleet should move, being thus always ready either to meet or to make an attack. In naval, as in military tactics, the formations for action depend on various conditions; on the localities, on moral circumstances, on national character, and on the talents of the commanders; and it is justly observed by a great tactician[a] that it is a fatal error to attempt the reduction of every system of war to fixed rules, and to cast as it were, in one mould, all the tactical combinations which a General may have to form.

168. On land, an enemy in retreat takes advantage of the inequalities of the ground, profits by the concealment which woods and other impediments to pursuit afford, and avails himself of the natural defences which are to be found in all countries : a limit is also assigned to the intensity of pursuit by an exhaustion of the physical energies of men and horses who have borne the heat and burden of the day. But the sphere of naval operation is an expanse of water open to view, except when ships are enveloped in smoke ; the manner and direction in which a discomfited fleet retires are seen, and the damage sustained is obvious. The seaman, his exertions in battle over, finds rest in his turn, and is restored to strength by an immediate supply of food, whilst his ship carries him forward to reap the fruits of the victory gained. It follows that an admiral of a steam-fleet who has succeeded in throwing an enemy's fleet into confusion, or in gaining a victory in the tactical signification of the term, will only have accomplished half his duty if he do not follow up his successes vigorously. Any advantage gained by a steam-fleet in action should always be attended with great results.

---

[a] Jomini, *Sur la Formation des Troupes*, 1815.

APPENDIX.

APPENDIX.

(A.)

LIST OF THE BRITISH STEAM NAVY.

	Guns.	H.P.		Guns.	H.P.
ABOUKIR, screw	90	400	Canadian, screw (nearly		
Agamemnon do.	91	600	ready for being launched)	17	..
Ajax do.	60	450	Caradoc, paddle	2	350
Alacrity, screw gun-vessel	4	200	Centaur do. (iron) ..	6	540
Alban, paddle	4	100	Centurion, screw	80	400
Alecto do.	5	200	Challenger, screw corvette	20	..
Alert, screw	16	100	Charybdis, screw corvette		
Algiers do.	91	600	(nearly ready for being		
Amphion do.	34	300	launched)	21	..
Anson, screw (ordered) ..	91	..	Chesapeake, screw	50	400
Antelope, paddle (iron) ..	3	260	Clio, screw corvette ..	20	..
Archer, screw	14	204	Colossus, screw	80	400
Ardent, paddle..	5	200	Columbia, paddle	6	100
Argus do.	6	300	Comet do.	3	80
Ariadne, screw (nearly			Conflict, screw	8	400
ready for being launched)	32	..	Conqueror do.	101	800
Ariel, screw..	9	60	Coquette, screw gun-vessel	4	200
Arrogant do.	46	360	Cordelia, screw	8	..
Arrow do.	4	160	Cormorant, screw gun-		
Assurance do.	4	200	vessel	4	200
Aurora do. (nearly ready			Cornwallis, screw	60	200
for being launched) ..	50	400	Cossack, screw corvette ..	20	250
Atlas, screw (nearly ready			Cressy, screw	80	400
for being launched) ..	91	800	Cruiser do.	17	60
Avon, paddle	3	60	Cuckoo, paddle	3	100
			Curaçoa, screw	30	350
			Curlew do.	9	60
Bacchante, screw ..	50	..	Cyclops, paddle	6	320
Banshee, paddle	3	350			
Barracouta do.	6	300	Dasher do.	2	100
Basilisk do.	6	400	Dauntless, screw	33	580
Beagle, screw	4	160	Dee, paddle	4	200
Blenheim do.	60	450	Defiance, screw (nearly		
Bloodhound, paddle (iron)	3	150	ready for being launched)	91	800
Brisk, screw	14	250	Desperate, screw	8	400
Brunswick do.	80	400	Devastator, paddle	6	50
Bulldog, paddle	6	500	Diadem, screw	34	800
Bulwark, screw (to be laid			Donegal do. (being built)	101	800
down)	91	..	Doris, screw	32	800
Buzzard, paddle	6	300	Dragon, paddle	6	560
			Driver do.	6	280
Cæsar, screw	90	400	Duncan, screw (nearly		
Cadmus, screw corvette ..	20		ready for being launched)	101	800
Camelion do. sloop ..	16		Duke of Wellington, screw	131	700

	Guns.	H. P.		Guns.	H. P.
Edgar, screw	91	600	Jason, screw (nearly ready		
Edinburgh, screw	60	450	for being launched) ..	21	..
Emerald do.	50	600			
Encounter do.	14	360	Kite, paddle	3	170
Eryalus do.	51	400			
Esk, screw corvette	21	250	Leopard, paddle	18	300
Exmouth, screw	91	400	Liffy, screw	50	600
Falcon do.	17	100	Lightning, paddle	3	100
Fawn do.	16	100	Lion, screw	80	400
Firebrand, paddle	6	410	Lizard, paddle (iron) ..	1	150
Firefly do.	4	420	Locust do.	3	100
Flying-fish, screw gun-			Lucifer do.	2	180
vessel	6	350	Lynx, screw	4	160
Forte, screw	50	400	Lyra do.	8	60
Forth do.	12	200			
Fox, screw transport ..	42	200	Magicienne, paddle ..	16	400
Furious, paddle	16	400	Majestic, screw	80	400
Fury do.	6	515	Malacca do.	17	200
			Marlborough, screw ..	131	800
Galatea, screw (nearly			Mars, screw	80	400
ready for being launched)	26	..	Meanee do.	80	400
Geyser, paddle..	6	280	Medea, paddle	6	350
Gibraltar, screw (nearly			Medina do.	4	312
ready for being launched)	101	800	Megæra, screw (iron) ..	6	350
Gladiator, paddle	6	430	Merlin, paddle	6	312
Goliah, screw	80	400	Miranda, screw	14	250
Gorgon, paddle	6	320	Mutine do. (nearly ready		
Greyhound, screw	17	..	for being launched) ..	17	100
			Myrmidon, paddle (iron)	3	150
Hannibal, screw	91	450			
Harpy, paddle (iron) ..	1	200	Neptune, screw (cut down)	90	..
Harrier, screw	17	100	Niger, screw	14	400
Hastings do.	60	200	Nile do.	91	560
Hawke do.	60	200			
Hecate, paddle	6	240	Oberon, paddle (iron) ..	3	260
Hecla do.	6	240	Odin, paddle	16	560
Hermes do.	6	220	Orion, screw	91	600
Hero, screw	91	600	Orpheus, screw (nearly		
Highflyer, screw corvette	21	250	ready for being launched)	22	..
Hogue, screw	60	450	Otter, paddle	3	120
Hood, screw (nearly ready					
for being launched) ..	91	600	Pearl, screw corvette ..	20	400
Horatio, screw	12	250	Pelican, screw (nearly		
Hornet do.	17	100	ready for being launched)	16	100
Howe, screw (nearly ready			Pelorus, screw corvette ..	20	..
for being launched) ..	121	1000	Pembroke, screw	60	200
Hydra, paddle	6	220	Penelope, paddle	16	650
			Perseverance, screw (iron)	2	360
Icarus, screw (nearly ready			Phœnix, screw	6	260
for being launched) ..	11	60	Pigmy, paddle	3	100
Immortalité, screw (nearly			Plumper, screw	9	60
ready for being launched)	50	..	Pluto, paddle	4	100
Impérieuse, screw	51	360	Porcupine, paddle	3	142
Industry, screw (iron) ..	2	80	Prince of Wales, screw		
Inflexible, paddle	6	370	(nearly ready for being		
Irresistible, screw (nearly			launched)	131	800
ready for being launched)	80	400	Princess Royal, screw ..	91	400
Jackall, paddle (iron) ..	4	150	Prometheus, paddle.. ..	5	200
James Watt, screw	91.	600	Pylades, screw corvette ..	20	350

	Guns.	H. P.		Guns.	H. P.
Queen, screw (cut down)	90	..	Stromboli, paddle (troop-ship)	6	280
Racoon, screw corvette ..	22	400			
Rattler, screw (broken up)	11	200	Styx, paddle	6	280
Renard, screw	4	200	Swallow, screw	9	60
Renown do.	91	800			
Retribution, paddle	28	400	Tartar, screw corvette ..	20	250
Revenge, screw (being built)	91	800	Tartarus, paddle	4	130
			Termagant, screw	24	310
Rhadamanthus, paddle ..	4	200	Terrible, paddle	21	800
Rosamond, paddle	6	280	Topaze, screw	50	..
Royal Albert, screw ..	121	500	Torch, paddle (iron) ..	..	150
Royal Frederick, screw (nearly ready for being launched)	116	..	Tribune, screw	31	300
			Trident, paddle (iron) ..	6	360
			Triton do. do. ..	3	250
Royal George, screw ..	102	400	Trafalgar (to be converted to a screw)	91	..
Royal Sovereign, screw ..	131	800			
Russell, screw	60	200	Valorous, paddle	16	400
St. Jean d'Acre, screw ..	101	600	Vesuvius do.	6	280
Salamander, paddle	6	220	Victor Emanuel, screw ..	91	600
Sampson, do.	6	467	Victoria, screw (nearly ready for being launched)	121	1000
San Fiorenzo, screw ..	50				
Sanspareil, screw	70	400	Victoria and Albert, paddle	2	600
Satellite, screw corvette ..	20	400	Viper, screw	4	160
Scourge, paddle	6	420	Virgo, paddle	6	300
Scout, screw corvette ..	20	400	Vivid do.	2	160
Scylla do. ..	20	400	Vixen do.	6	280
Seahorse do. ..	12	200	Volcano do.	3	140
Shannon, screw	51	600	Vulcan, screw	6	350
Shearwater, paddle	8	160	Vulture, paddle	6	470
Sidon, paddle	22	560			
Simoom, screw (iron) ..	8	350	Wasp, screw	14	100
Snake, screw	4	160	Windsor Castle, screw ..	101	..
Sparrowhawk, screw ..	4	200	Wrangler, screw	4	160
Sphinx, paddle	6	500			
Spiteful do.	6	280	Zealous, screw (ordered)	91	..
Spitfire do.	5	140	Zephyr do.	3	100

Thus the British steam navy consists of—

    32 Steamers, of 90 guns and upwards.
    32   ,,   50 to 90 guns.
    27   ,,   20 to 50 guns.
  127   ,,   20 and under.

There are, besides, 186 steam gun-boats, with engines varying from 20 to 60 horse-power; and 40 steam-vessels consisting of tenders, store-ships, and tugs.

The 'Renown' is our best screw-steamer, and should be the model of those to be hereafter constructed. At present we have few like her.

(B.)

WAR NAVIES OF THE SEVERAL CONTINENTAL POWERS OF EUROPE, AND OF THE UNITED STATES.

The number of French ships of the line and vessels of war, when the Commission of Inquiry (Enquête Parlementaire) commenced its labours, in 1850, was as in the following table :—

	Afloat.	On the Stocks.
Ships of the line	27	20
Frigates	30	18
Corvettes	31	3
Brigs	46	
Gun-brigs	6	
Batimens légers	33	
Sailing transports	37	
Steam-ships of war, from 450 to 650 H. P...	20	
Ditto, from 220 to 400 H. P.	27	
Ditto, of 200 H. P. and under	60	

The twenty-seven ships of the line afloat are as follow :—

First-rate .. ..
- Ocean.
- Montebello.   Auxiliary (150 H. P.)
- Souverain.
- *Friedland.
- *Valmy.
- *Ville de Paris.

Second-rate .. ..
- *Hercule.
- *Jemappes.
- *Tage.
- *Henri Quatre.

Third-rate .. ..
- Jena.
- *Suffrein.
- *Inflexible.
- *Bayard.
- *Duguesclin.
- *Breslau.
- Charlemagne.   Auxiliary (256 H. P.)
- Diadème.
- Neptune.
- Jupiter.
- Napoléon.   Steamer (960 H. P.)

Fourth-rate .. ..
- Marengo.
- Trident.
- Ville de Marseille.
- Alger.
- Duperré.
- Généreux.

* Those marked with an asterisk were to be immediately converted into steam ships.

The twenty ships said to be then on the stocks are as follow :—

First-rate   ..   ..   Louis Quatorze.

Second-rate ..   ..   {
Fleurus.
Ulm.
Duguay Trouin.
Annibal.
Turenne.
Navarin.
Austerlitz.   Steamer.
Wagram.
Eylau.

Third-rate   ..   ..   {
Donawerth.
Fontenoy.
Tilsit.
Massena.
Castiglione.
Duquesne.
Tourville.
Saint Louis.
Alexandre.
Jean Bart.   Steamer.

Eighteen of the above twenty were sailing ships, and these have since been converted into steamers. The twelve old sailing-ships, marked above with an asterisk, have since been lengthened and are to be converted into screw-steamers of 400 to 450 horse-power. All these will, when finished, make thirty-two line-of-battle steamers; but, since that time, twelve new steam-ships have been built, and one of these, the 'Bretagne,' was launched at Cherbourg, on the opening of that port in the present year: it carries 131 guns, and has engines of 1000 horse-power. The building of new ships in the ports of France continues, and there is no doubt that in 1861 the number will amount to fifty, as recommended by a member of the "Commission of Inquiry," in 1851. All the new ships of the line are built on the type of the 'Napoléon,' and are to have engines of nearly equal horse-power.

It may be interesting to know that, according to the evidence given at the *Enquête Parlementaire* in 1851, the total quantity of oak timber, for the purpose of ship-building, then in store at the five great ports of France—Cherbourg, Brest, L'Orient, Rochfort, and Toulon—amounted to 207,673 stère (7,334,387 cubic feet), and of fir 28,831 stère (1,018,224 cubic feet); also that the whole mean annual consumption of oak for this purpose, at the same ports, was 35,834 stère, or 1,265,549 cubic feet.

STATE OF THE FRENCH NAVY IN MAY, 1858.

CLASSES.	AFLOAT.			BUILDING.			TOTALS.
	Steam.	Sail.	Total.	Steam.	Sail.	Total.	
Ships of the line	30	13	43	7	..	7	50
Frigates	37	28	65	2	11	13	78
Corvettes	18	11	29	3	3	6	35
Brigs	..	23	23	..	2	2	25
Avisos	83	..	83	10	..	10	93
Floating batteries	5	..	5	..	..	..	5
Gun-boats	28	..	28	..	..	..	28
Mortar-ships	..	3	3	..	..	..	3
Small vessels	..	..	31	..	..	..	31
Screw transports	20	..	20	6	..	6	26
Transports	..	26	26	..	..	..	26
Total	221	135	356	28	16	44	400

The Russian navy, during the war with Turkey in 1829, consisted of five divisions, each comprehending 9 line-of-battle ships, 6 frigates, and 8 corvettes and brigs, with 8 steamers. This force has since been augmented to 12 line-of-battle ships in each division. The total establishment of the Russian fleet at the commencement of the late war was 60 ships of the line, armed with from 70 to 120 guns; 37 frigates, of from 40 to 60 guns; 70 corvettes and brigs; 40 steamers and 200 gun-boats. The system of manning is by establishments of *équipages de ligne*, as in France. (See Art. 35, note, *Naval Gunnery*, 4th edition.) Of this vast naval force three-fifths were stationed in the Baltic, and two-fifths in the Black Sea. These last divisions having been destroyed, and treaty obligations having been forced upon Russia not to re-establish a naval arsenal at Sebastopol, she is devoting her naval resources to increase her Baltic fleet, which will, in the course of the next year, amount to 40 steam ships of the line, all the sailing ships being converted into steamers.

The Austrian navy consists of—

2 Ships of the line.
6 Frigates, carrying 215 guns.
5 Corvettes,   ,,   92   ,,
7 Brigs,   ,,   112   ,,
6 Schooners,   ,,   58   ,,
2 Prams,   ,,   20   ,,

1 Gun-boat, carrying 10 guns.
34 Pinnaces   ,,   102   ,,
18 Sloops   ,,   60   ,,
5 Schooner-brigs   12   ,,
11 Steamers   ,,   64   ,,
5 Trabacotis.

The navy of the Netherlands consisted, in 1850, of—

2	Ships of	..	84 guns.	4	Ships of	..	22 guns.
5	,,	..	74 ,,	2	,,	..	20 ,,
3	,,	..	60 ,,	10	,,	..	18 ,,
1	,,	..	54 ,,	9	,,	..	14 ,,
8	,,	..	44 ,,	3	,,	..	15 ,,
2	,,	..	38 ,,	10	,,	..	12 ,,
2	,,	..	28 ,,	1	,,	..	8 ,,
4	,,	..	26 ,,	11	,,	6, 5, or 4 ,,

There are, besides,—

18	Steamers of	7	guns.
1	,,	8	,,
2	,,	4	,,

Six sailing-ships and three steamers-of-war were on the stocks.

The Dutch navy, under the ministry of Admiral Gobins, an experienced and excellent officer, is in a very efficient state.

The Danish navy, in 1853, consisted of—

		Guns.
5 Line-of-battle-Ships	.. .. ..	66 to 84
7 Frigates	.. .. ..	44 to 60
3 Corvettes	.. .. ..	20 to 28
4 Brigs..	.. .. ..	12 to 16
1 Barque	.. .. ..	12
3 Schooners..	.. .. ..	1 to 3
1 Cutter	.. .. ..	6 falconets.
38 Gun-sloops and Boats	.. .. ..	1 to 2

Steam-vessels as follow :—

	Guns.		H. P.
Thor	12	30-pr.	260
Holger Danske ..	1	60-pr., 6 30-pr. ..	260
Heckla	1	60-pr., 6 24-pr. ..	200
Geiser	2	60-pr., 6 18-pr. ..	160
Skirner	2	24-pr.	120
Ægir	2	18-pr.	80

There were then on the stocks—

	Guns.		H. P.
1 Steam-frigate ..	44	30 pr.	300
1 Corvette	16		

The Swedish navy, in 1852, consisted of—

10 Line-of-battle-Ships.	8 Schooners.
6 Frigates.	214 Gun-boats.
4 Corvettes.[a]	7 Mortar-boats.
1 Brig.	21 Advice-boats.

There are, besides, 10 steam-vessels.

Of the ten line-of-battle ships, two are said to be in bad condition and the remaining six were to be fitted to receive screw-propellers.

The Norwegian naval force consists of—

3 Frigates.
4 Corvettes.
1 Brig.

			Guns.
3 Schooners, carrying	..		68-pr.
2 Do.	,,	..	24-pr.
80 Gun-boats,	,,	2	68-pr.
40 Gun-yawls	,,	2	24-pr.

There is, besides, 1 steam-corvette.

THE UNITED STATES' NAVY.

From the Report of the Secretary of the Navy in 1856.

Wabash, steam-frigate.	James Town, sloop.
Merrimac do.	St. Louis do.
Niagara do.	Dale do.
Susquehanna do.	Levant do.
Minnesota do.	Portsmouth do.
Saranac do.	Powhattan, steam-frigate.
San Jacinto do.	Macedonian, sloop-of-war.
Savannah.	Vandalia do.
Resolute.	Independence, frigate.
Fulton.	John Adams, sloop.
St. Lawrence.	St. Mary do.
Saratoga, sloop-of-war.	Decator do.
Cyane.	Massachusetts, steamer.
Germantown.	John Hancock do.
Falmouth.	Dolphin, brig.
Bainbridge.	Fennimore Cooper.
Water Witch.	Arctic, steamer.
Congress, frigate.	Plymouth, sloop-of-war.
Constellation, sloop-of-war.	Vincennes.

---

[a] One of these, the ' Naijaden ' (18 guns), is the exercising ship, for gunnery practice, in the Swedish navy. This vessel of war is now being repaired in Chatham dock, having sustained considerable damage by running aground on the Galloper Sands during her voyage from Christiansund, on her way to the West Indies.

The armament of five new frigates consists of 8, 9, 10, and 11-inch shell guns. The 8-inch guns are on the spar-deck, and the 9-inch guns on the gun-deck : the frigates have besides a 68-pounder solid-shot pivot-gun at bow and stern, the 10-inch shell-gun, which was formed upon the model of the 10-inch British shell-gun, having been abolished in the United States navy, as being deficient in accuracy, range, and power.[a] Yet this very defective shell-gun, displaced, as a pivot-gun, in the British service, on account of its great inferiority to the 68-pounder solid-shot gun, as shown in Article 268, p. 258, 'Naval Gunnery,' and wholly proscribed from the naval service of the United States, forms the principal armament of the ' Diadem,' and other frigates of her class, lately built and armed, as fully equal to contend with the United States frigate ' Niagara,' ' Merrimac,' &c.! Surely this defective shell-gun should be forthwith withdrawn, and the 68-pounder solid-shot gun substituted. There is ample displacement and deck-room to admit of this ; and we have the authority of Captain Dahlgren, and even that of the gallant Captain of the ' Diadem,' for asserting, that the 95-cwt. solid-shot 68-pounder may be worked as easily as a 32-pounder, and, it may be added, fired at long ranges with solid shot, as rapidly, at least, as a 10-inch shell-gun, which cannot fire solid shot.

The ' Niagara ' carries twelve 11-inch guns, each capable of throwing a shell weighing 135 lbs. All the shell-guns are capable of firing solid shot ; but in the United States' service hollow shot are abolished.[b] Shells are preferred on account of the destructive effects which are expected to ensue when they explode in an enemy's ship.

It has been recommended to the Government of the United States that there should be constructed a number of sloops of war, each furnished with brass boat-guns—12 and 24-pounders. These vessels, on account of their small draught of water, are expected to do good service in defending the coasts, or on entering an enemy's harbours.

---

[a] Dahlgren, ' Shells and Shell-guns,' pp. 35, 255.
[b] Ibid., p. 21.

(C.)

ON THE FORMATION OF A NEW CODE OF NAVAL TACTICS.

A COMMITTEE of the most scientific and experienced Naval officers, with the aid of some officers of the Artillery and Engineers, well versed in tactical science, and in the arts of military attack and defence, should be appointed, in order to make a selection of formations adapted to fleets composed exclusively of steamers; and to decide upon the evolutions to be performed by such fleets previously to, and during the continuance of, an action at sea. A measure of this kind is now become one of paramount importance, and even of absolute necessity; since, as has been already stated in this work (Arts. 40, 97, 102, 112, 113), the motive powers of steam and wind cannot be made to act together without entirely nullifying, through the limitations imposed by the wind, and the complexity of the operations, the advantages which are to be derived from the application of steam being made with equal facility in all the various conditions of naval warfare.

In the presence of an enemy at sea, all sails must be furled, and the Regulations relating to warfare under sail must be disregarded. Others of a different character must be prepared; and even a vocabulary of terms must be provided, in accordance with the new system of tactics, as substitutes for the technicalities relating to the movements, and the working of sailing ships; these will have no place in the tactics of steam fleets, and ought, in consequence, to become obsolete. In a steam ship there will be no starboard or larboard tack; the more simple terms right or left will suffice: there will be no luffing up or wearing round; and the order to turn ship in an assigned direction, communicated by signal or otherwise, may be given in their stead; and the like may be said of many other nautical phrases, which, henceforth, should be considered as antiquated, and should give place to others more in accordance with ordinary language. The circumstances of armies in the field have their analogues in naval warfare; therefore, military terms might with advantage be introduced in nautical science; and thus the inconvenience of employing different terms to designate similar actions or objects would be avoided.

It appears to the author that a committee of the most scientific and experienced officers of the Royal, and Royal Marine Artillery, that can be obtained, should also be appointed to revise the Regulations which now exist respecting the armament of the British line-of-battle steam ships, with a view of adapting the armament to the volumes of the ships, and keeping it in harmony with the great tactical principle of reciprocal defence. In carrying out this principle, the gunnery powers of the different ships require to be combined with each other in such a manner as to give the greatest military strength to the whole fleet, by enabling each ship to give to, and receive from, the neighbouring ships, that support which constitutes the main strength of a defensive system, instead of, as in times past, leaving each ship to rely on its own isolated strength.

When a special code of Regulations for the evolutions of steam fleets shall have been completed, a new code of signals, by which the regulations for executing those evolutions may be most effectually carried into effect, should also be drawn up. The same distinctive signal flags as are at present in use, may be employed; but they should be displayed in a different manner. Flags droop in calm weather, which is the most propitious time for an engagement between steam fleets, and then they become useless; even when they flutter in the breeze they are not easily made out, if the wind should be in the direction in which the signal is to be made. Every signal flag should therefore be bent to two small yards, one above and the other below, an expedient often put in practice during the late wars, but which should now be invariably adopted: the flags should be connected together in the prescribed combination; hoisted to the most conspicuous part of the rigging, their planes perpendicular to the direction in which the signal is to be passed.

INDEX.

INDEX TO THE WORDS,

ALPHABETICALLY ARRANGED.

L

W.

	PAGE.	ARTICLE.
Watt, patent for the improved steam-engine taken out by	22	2
Wheel and screw, points to be attended to in finding the relative capabilities of the	53	58
Wheel, locomotive powers of the, greater than those of a screw with an equal consumption of fuel..	59	68
Widgeon and Archimedes, experimental trial by the ..	50	50
Wladimir, steam-power of the	46	45
Windward position, advantage of the, for sailing ships	80	92

Y.

	PAGE.	ARTICLE.
Yokes employed for steering screw-steamers	54–67	60–97

LONDON : PRINTED BY WILLIAM CLOWES AND SONS, STAMFORD STREET, AND CHARING-CROSS.

For EU product safety concerns, contact us at Calle de José Abascal, 56–1°,
28003 Madrid, Spain or eugpsr@cambridge.org.

www.ingramcontent.com/pod-product-compliance
Ingram Content Group UK Ltd.
Pitfield, Milton Keynes, MK11 3LW, UK
UKHW012340130625
459647UK00009B/422